PENELOPE ROSKELL'S COMPLETE PIANIST SERIES

Essential Piano Technique

LEVEL 2

Late elementary

by
Penelope Roskell

Original music by Aaron Burrows

ALLE RECHTE VORBEHALTEN · ALL RIGHTS RESERVED
EDITION PETERS
PUBLISHED BY FABER MUSIC
Leipzig · London · New York

Author acknowledgements

These books would not have been possible without the support of many friends and colleagues. In particular I would like to thank:

Huei Flowers, Clare Spencer, Panos Messis, Inês Costa, Louissa Galenski, Monika Walo, Richard Dinsmore, Hannah O'Toole, Anuvrat Choudhary, Dr Oliver Griffiths and members of the Roskell Academy.

This edition © 2025 by Faber Music Ltd
Brownlow Yard, 12 Roger Street, London WC1N 2JU
Cover portrait of Penelope Roskell by kind permission of John Batten
Page design by Liz Ogden
Illustrations by Eilidh Muldoon and Liz Ogden
Music setting by John Rogers
Video production by Informance
Printed in England by Caligraving Ltd
All rights reserved

ISMN 979-0-57702-487-5

Contents

	Hello!		4
Getting started	Introduction		5
	Circle warm-ups		6
	Sitting posture		7
Hand positions	Hand positions old and new	*Patchwork Polka*	8
Rounded movements	Circular movements	*Orbit*	12
	Hand gym		15
Strengthening exercises	Strengthening the weaker fingers		16
	Playing with 4 and 5	*Study in A minor* (Gurlitt)	17
Rounded movements	More rounded movements	*Gigue* (Arnold)	19
Black notes	Thumb on a black note	*Whimsy*	22
Tone control	Sound explorer		23
	Matching hands	*Sliding on the Ice* (Beach)	24
	Legato-staccato	*Frère Jacques*	27
		Chasing the Sloth (Gurlitt)	29
		Calypso	30
	Left-hand melodies	*In the Garden* (Gurlitt)	31
Scales	New major scales		33
	Expressive scales	*Mini-Mozart*	35
		Daydream	37
Rotation	Alberti bass	*Sonatine* (Attwood)	38
	Broken thirds	*Thirdly*	40
Scales	Harmonic minor scales	*Waltz*	41
Arpeggios	The elbow spa		43
	One-octave arpeggios	*As the Wind Cries*	44
Leaps	Crossing hands	*Loading Screen*	47
Pedalling	Pedal explorer		48
	Legato pedalling	*Pachelbel's Canon*	49
		The Lonely Gondolier	51
	Combining techniques	*Sonatina* (Clementi)	52
		Broadway	54
	Teaching notes		60

Hello!

Welcome to Level 2 in the *Essential Piano Technique* series. Here you will learn:

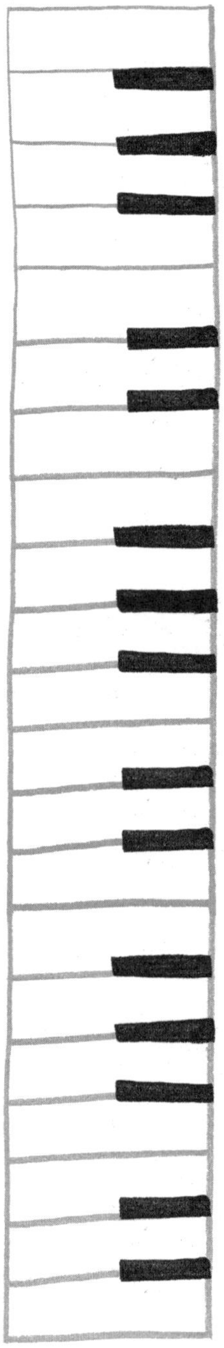

- New warm-ups
- How to create a wide range of sound through sound explorer activities
- How to play expressively with rounded movements
- Arpeggios and harmonic minor scales in lots of new keys
- Coordinating the hands with mixed articulation
- Left-hand melodies and *Alberti bass*
- *Legato* pedalling

There is also a wonderful selection of new pieces for you to play. When practising, remind yourself of the Practice Pointers and Technique Tips. If you would like to explore some of the techniques further, check out the extension activites 》 and also some of the specially selected related pieces.

If you are new to this series, you may find it helpful to revise some of the fundamental techniques from the previous books, especially the Parachute touch, Down-ups and the Skipping-rope technique (from Primer B); and Jellyfish jumps, Rotation and Legato pedalling (from Level 1).

You can access the video demonstrations via the QR code, or by visiting www.fabermusic.com/ep/essential-piano-technique.

Introduction

To the teacher

This is the fourth book in the *Essential Piano Technique* series. It develops many of the techniques studied in the previous books, as well as introducing new techniques. On completing the book, students will have learnt the techniques they need to play pieces at the late elementary level (around Grade 2) confidently and with ease.

Much of the focus of Level 2 is on awareness of piano sound and playing expressively. Students are encouraged to listen carefully, develop sensitivity of touch and play with gestures that bring out the expressive quality of each exercise or piece.

Students who are new to this series will benefit from looking at some of the fundamental techniques from previous books in the *Essential Piano Technique* series, especially Rainbows, the Parachute touch, Down-ups, Jellyfish jumps, the Skipping-rope technique, Rotation and Legato pedalling.

Each technique is put into practice in simple exercises, followed by studies and pieces. Each technique can be explored further, using creative activities of your own devising, or the optional extension activities.

Some pieces are short or have been arranged so the student can learn the notes quickly while focusing almost exclusively on the techniques being studied. The longer pieces may be seen as performance pieces which will be studied over a longer period of time. The progression has been planned very carefully to guide your student successfully through all the challenges encountered at this level. However, at times you may feel the need to adopt a flexible approach and dip in and out of chapters as and when the need arises.

Tempo markings have been intentionally omitted. Students should start each example at a steady speed and only increase the tempo once the technique feels secure.

Explanations of the learning objectives, more detailed teaching tips and further suggestions for related pieces are available in the Teaching Notes at the back of the book. These Teaching Notes can be supplemented by accessing the Roskell Academy website (www.roskellacademy.com) which offers teachers supporting material and access to training and certification in the Roskell method. You can also find more information about each aspect of technique in *The Complete Pianist: from healthy technique to natural artistry* (Edition Peters, 2020).

Circle warm-ups

Here's a warm-up sequence you can do every day before you sit down to play. These exercises will help you relax your shoulders and arms and get your blood flowing. You'll also be able to play more quickly and easily when your arms are warm and relaxed.

Empty sleeves
Twist your body from side to side, letting your arms swing loosely around your body.

Windmills
Draw huge windmills from your shoulders!

Shoulder rolls
Place your right hand lightly on your right shoulder and your left hand on your left shoulder. Bring your elbows together then up and back in a circular motion. Breathe in as your elbows float up – breathe out as they float down.

Circling the thumbs
Draw a circle with your thumbs in one direction, then the other.

Wrist circles
Draw a circle with your hands, circling from your wrists in both directions.

Elbows
Draw a big circle from your elbows.

Wiping the table
Imagine you are wiping a big table in front of you or swimming breaststroke. Make BIG arm circles, then small ones.

Sitting posture

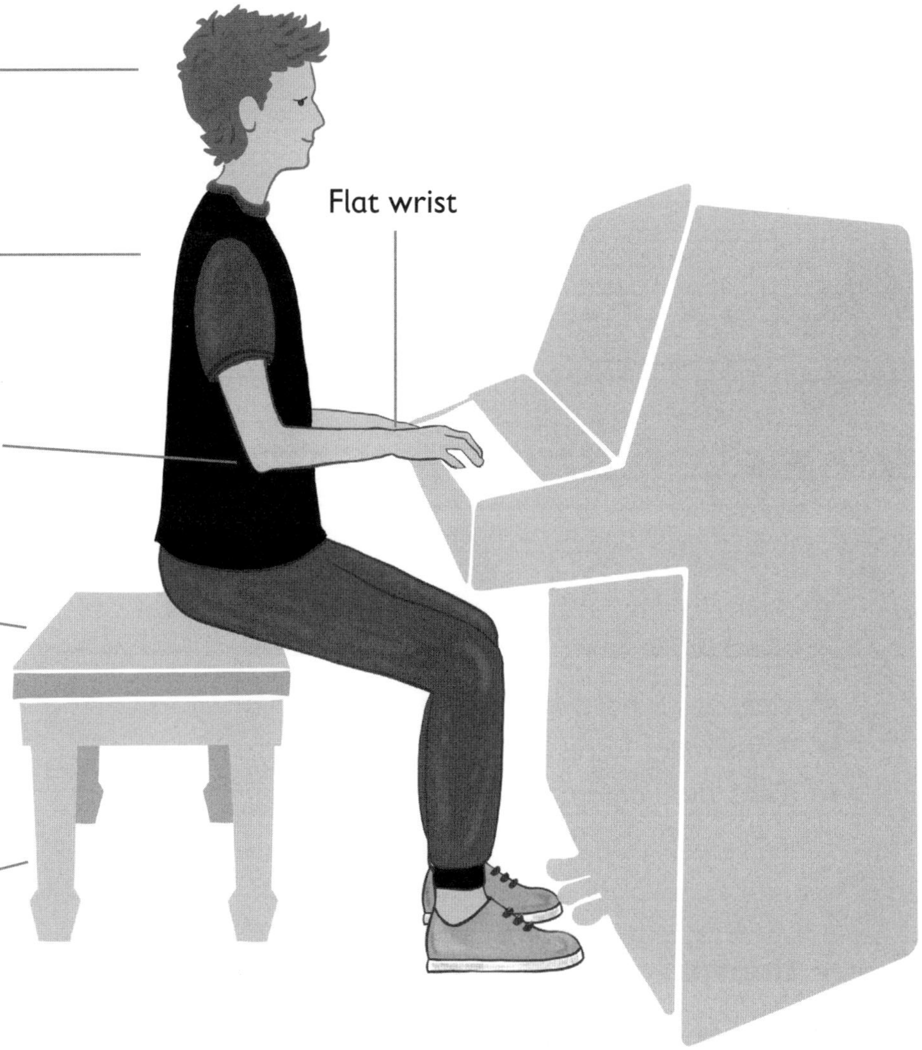

Sit tall

Flat wrist

Shoulders relaxed

Floppy elbows

Sit on the front half of the piano seat. Allow enough space between your body and the keyboard for your arms to move around freely.

Adjust the height of the seat so your forearm is roughly parallel to the floor, or sloping slightly downwards.

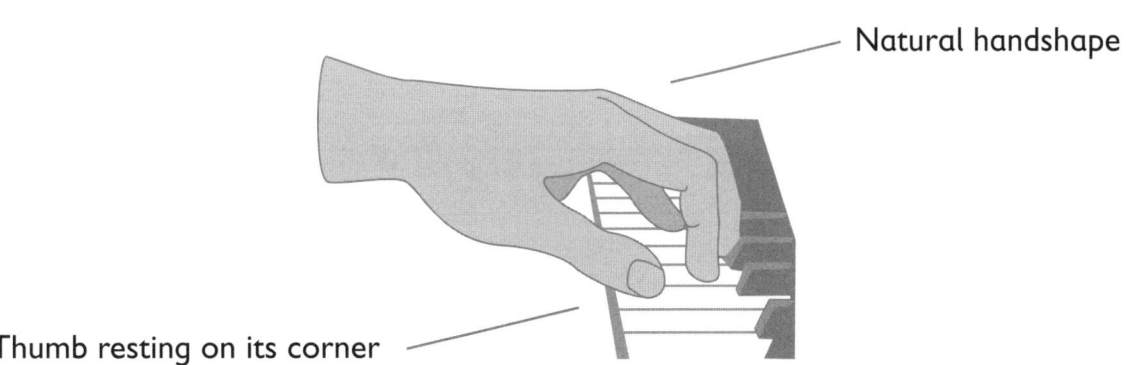

Natural handshape

Thumb resting on its corner

Hand positions old and new

In this chapter you will revise some hand positions, learn some new ones and then put them into practice in a fun piece. You will be able to recognise these hand positions whenever you see them in pieces in the future.

The Basic five-finger pattern

Start by playing the **Basic five-finger pattern** in C major:

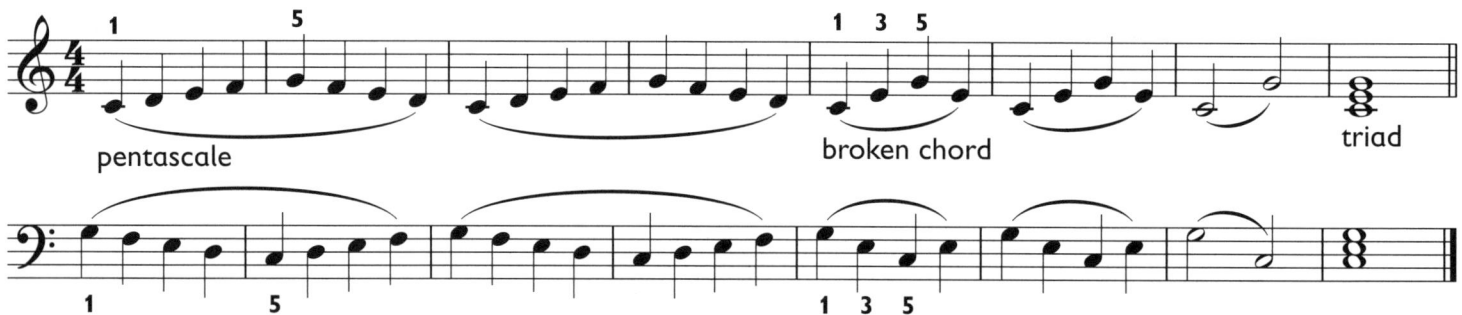

Technique Tips

✔ Keep a rounded handshape.
✔ Remember to rest your thumb on its corner.
✔ Parachute onto the first note.

Three themes

Then practise each of these themes in the C major hand position until you can play them from memory:

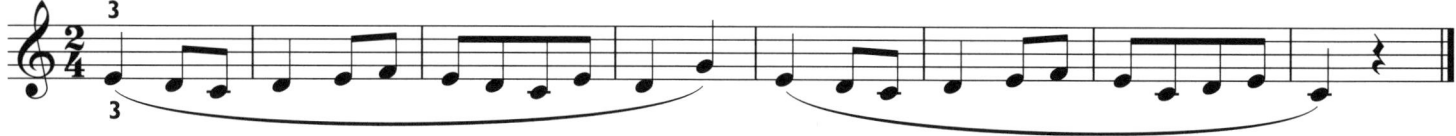

8

White-note keys

Now play the **Basic five-finger pattern** and all **Three themes** given on page 8 in each of these white-note keys. Play hands separately, then together.

G major   D minor   A minor

One black note

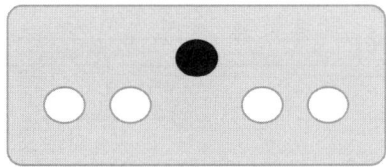

Now play the **Basic five-finger pattern** and the **Three themes** in the following keys. Move your hand forward a little so your middle finger can reach the black note comfortably without having to stretch out.

D major   A major   G minor   C minor

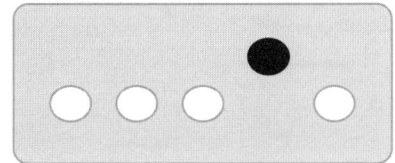

Then play the **Basic five-finger pattern** and **Three themes** in the **F major** hand position.

 **E major**

 Practise the **Basic five-finger pattern** in E major and B major. For B major you will have to move your whole hand forward so your fifth finger can reach the black note easily.

 **B major**

 Look out for pentascales, chords and broken chords in each piece you play.

Patchwork Polka, on the next page, repeats the **Three themes** in different keys. Look out for these techniques that were all discussed in Primer B:

Staccato   Down-ups   Longer slurs   Breathing wrist

Parachute touch   The elephant walk

PRIMO

Patchwork Polka

Pupil to play in octaves throughout, the right hand playing one octave higher than written.

Aaron Burrows

>> Now create your own Patchwork Polka, combining the three themes in different keys and in a different order.

You might also like:

Henry Purcell: 'Prelude in G' from *Suite No. 1*

Elissa Milne: 'Spiral Staircase' from *Very Easy Little Peppers*

11

Circular movements

If you play the piano just by moving your fingers, the music can sound flat and boring. Making flowing, rounded movements with your hands can bring the music to life.

Gluey finger circles

First start with some **Circle warm-ups** from page 6.

Now rest your third finger on your knee or on a flat surface. Imagine your fingertip is glued down and move your wrist round in big circles. Move your right hand and left hand in both directions, then hands together going in opposite directions. Start by making big circles, then smaller circles. Now try some gluey finger circles with your finger 'glued' to a piano key.

Up-and-overs

Use a low-to-high wrist to add a rounded movement to some familiar five-finger patterns. Play the passage below, starting with a low wrist and gradually raising it.

Now play the notes without stopping, using one continuous wrist movement. Does this phrase sound more expressive when you play it with a rounded movement?

Now play a pentascale on white notes. Feel your wrist turning like a big wheel, then a smaller wheel.

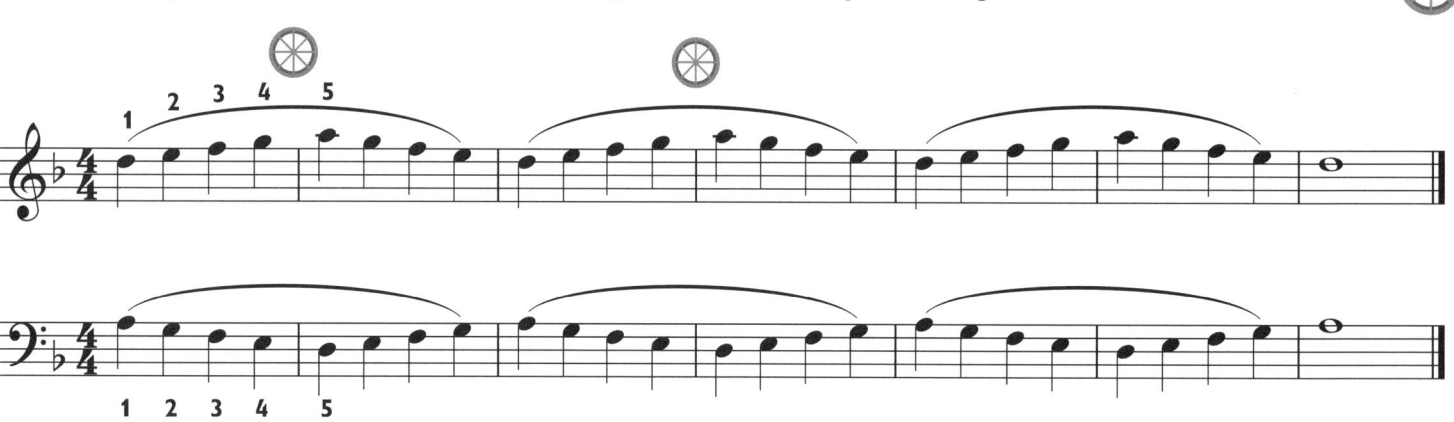

Spinning wheels

You can use the same circular wrist movements to play broken chords. Keep repeating the wrist circles until you can play **Spinning wheels** with ease.

Accel. is short for *accelerando* (pronounced *at-chell-er-an-do*) which means getting faster. How fast can you go in the *accelerando*?

As you play faster, the movement becomes smaller and more like a squashed wheel.

Now repeat the **Basic five-finger pattern** from the last chapter, incorporating **Up-and-overs** and **Spinning wheels**.

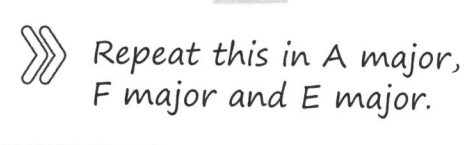

Repeat this in A major, F major and E major.

Orbit

Draw big circles at first then make them small and neat. Play as expressively as you can.

Andante

Aaron Burrows

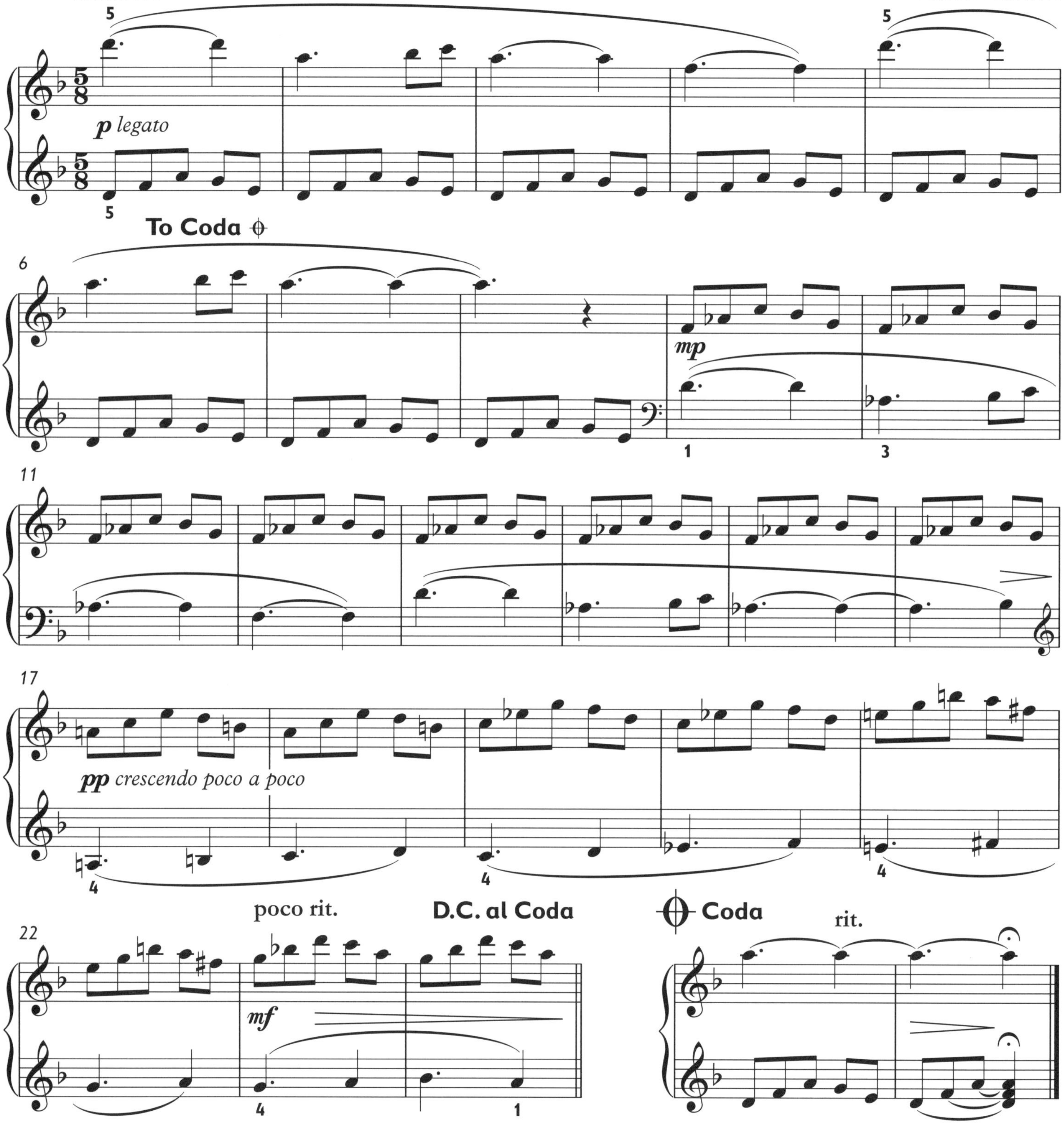

You might also like:

Friedrich Burgmüller: 'La Candeur' (No. 1) from *25 Easy and Progressive Studies* Op. 100

Florence Price: 'A Morning Sunbeam' from *Three Sketches for Little Pianists*

Hand gym

Itchy leg
Cup your hand over your knee. Scratch your leg with each fingernail in turn. Feel your finger bending at the end joint.

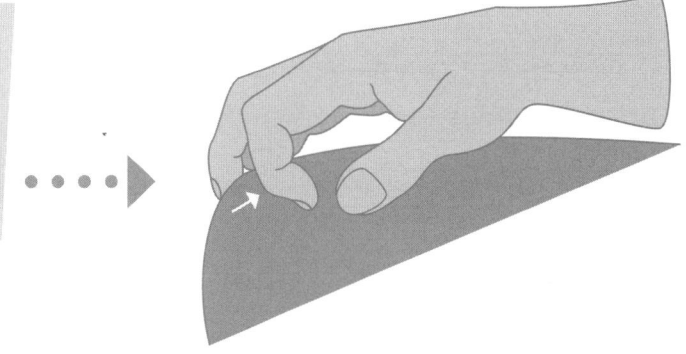

Snapping crocodile
Touch your thumb and second finger together like a crocodile opening and closing its mouth. Then snap your thumb against your third finger, then fourth finger.

Squeezing the circle
Form a circle between the tip of your thumb and second finger. Keep the circle round and count to 5 as you squeeze them gently together. Repeat with your third, then fourth finger.

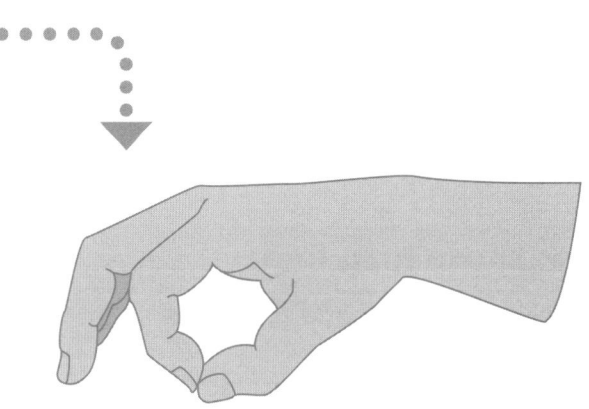

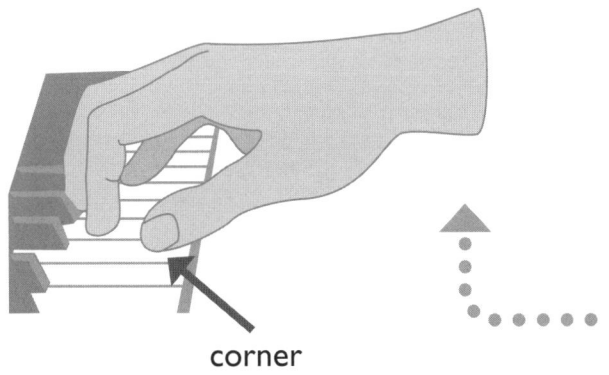

corner

Tapping thumb
Rest your hand on a table in playing position and tap lightly up and down with the corner of your thumb, being careful not to dip your wrist. Repeat at the piano.

Strengthening the weaker fingers

Do your fourth and fifth fingers feel weaker than the others? Here are some ways to strengthen them.

Itchy leg again
Repeat **Itchy leg** from page 15, focusing on your fourth and fifth fingers.

Wiggly spider legs
Rest the back of your hand on a flat surface like a sleepy spider. Relax your hand and arm. Gently wiggle your fifth finger like a spider leg, moving your finger from your knuckle. Repeat with your fourth finger. Wiggle your fingers at least ten times every day on each hand to strengthen those fingers.

Stretchy spider legs
Cup your hand over your knee like a floppy spider and relax your arm. Slide your fourth finger down your leg and back up again five times. Then slide your fifth finger down your leg and up five times. Practise this every day to make those fingers stronger, adding in one more stretch each day.

Walking on tiptoes
Using your third and fourth fingers, practise walking your hand forward along a table on your fingertips. Watch your nail turn down towards the table as you walk forwards. Then have a go with your fourth and fifth fingers.

Banish those lazy fingers!

Sometimes the fourth and fifth fingers can be a bit lazy and forget to lift at the end of a note.

Play a **Basic five-finger pattern** in A major. Listen carefully – do you hear any overlap between the notes? Do you have lazy fingers that stay down too long?

Repeat the pattern several times, making sure each finger lifts *as you press the next finger down*.

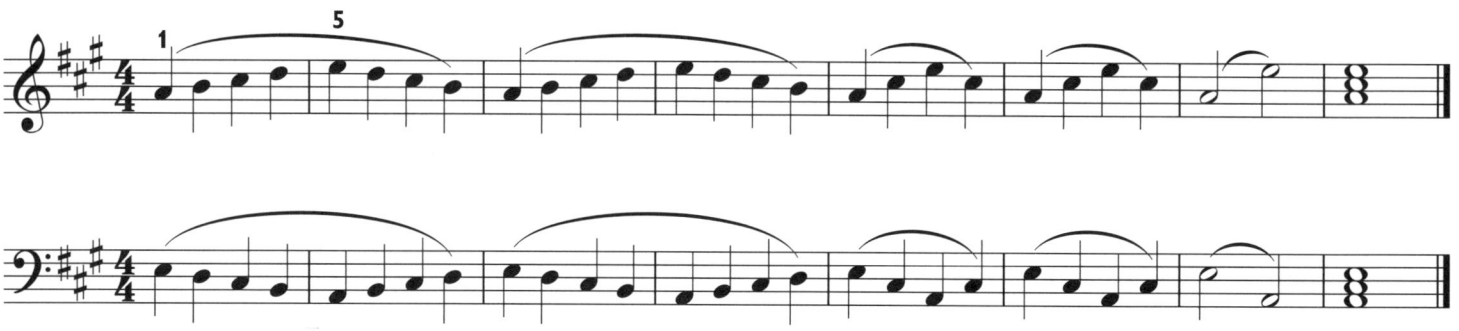

Playing with 4 and 5

Your fourth and fifth fingers will feel much stronger when you play with your arm lined up behind them!

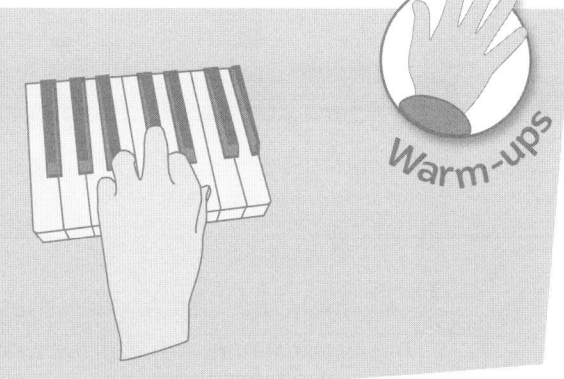

Lining up your arm

Rest your third finger lightly on a surface. Swing your wrist loosely from side to side. Come to rest in a position where your forearm is in a straight line with your fifth finger. Now tap your fifth finger on the surface. Does that feel fairly easy?

All lined up

Play the passage below starting with your arm in line with your fifth finger. Swivel your wrist towards the thumb as you play through fingers 4, 3, 2 and 1, then swivel back again as you move towards finger 5. Try big movements at first, then make the wrist movements smaller.

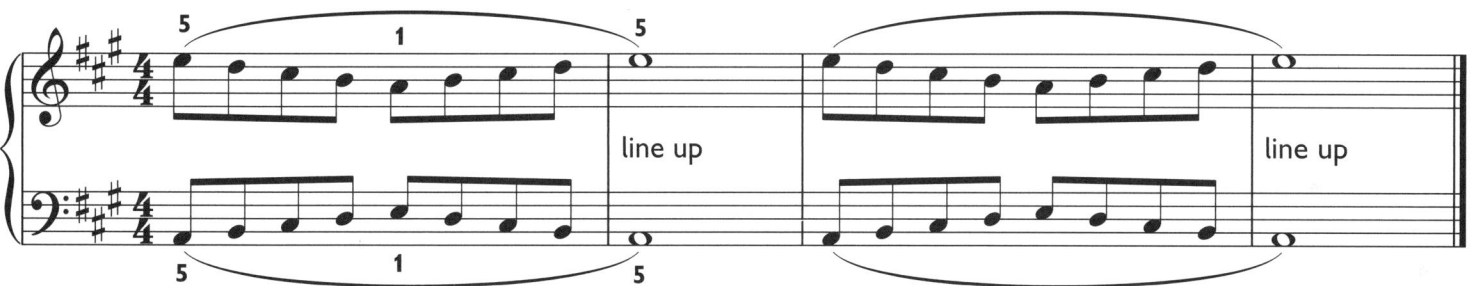

Now play the same exercise without lining up your arm – do your fourth and fifth fingers feel weaker when not in line?

Workout for fingers 4 and 5

On a flat surface, balance your hand on the tip of your fifth finger. Check that your arm is in line with your fifth finger. Then move onto your fourth finger. Keep walking gently from your fifth to your fourth finger. Keep a good hand position and a relaxed arm.

Now at the piano:

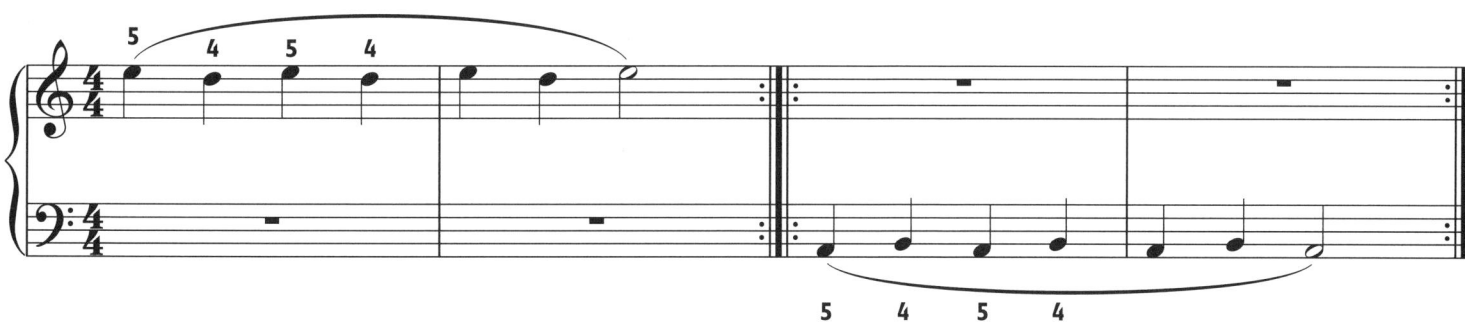

Spinning around

Add a small **Up-and-over** movement each time you play the fifth finger.

 **Technique Tips**
- ✔ Play the fifth finger lightly without pressing your whole hand downwards.
- ✘ No squashed spiders! Keep your rounded handshape.

Study in A minor

The natural sign ♮ cancels the sharp sign ♯ that came earlier in the bar. Remember to line up your arm with your fifth finger.

Cornelius Gurlitt
arr. Penelope Roskell

More rounded movements

Hand swirls

In these exercises, your hand swirls around the keyboard, making circular movements. Start slowly:

Then play faster circles:

Tumbleweed

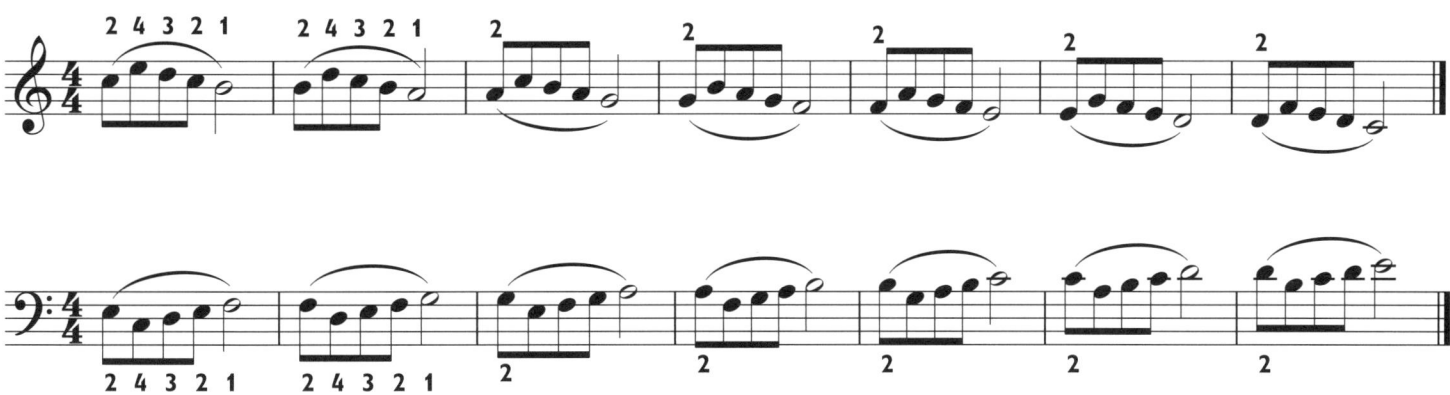

Now join the patterns together in a continuous motion. You will need to close your hand to bring the fourth finger into position. Can you hear a slight *diminuendo* within each circle?

Rounded movements

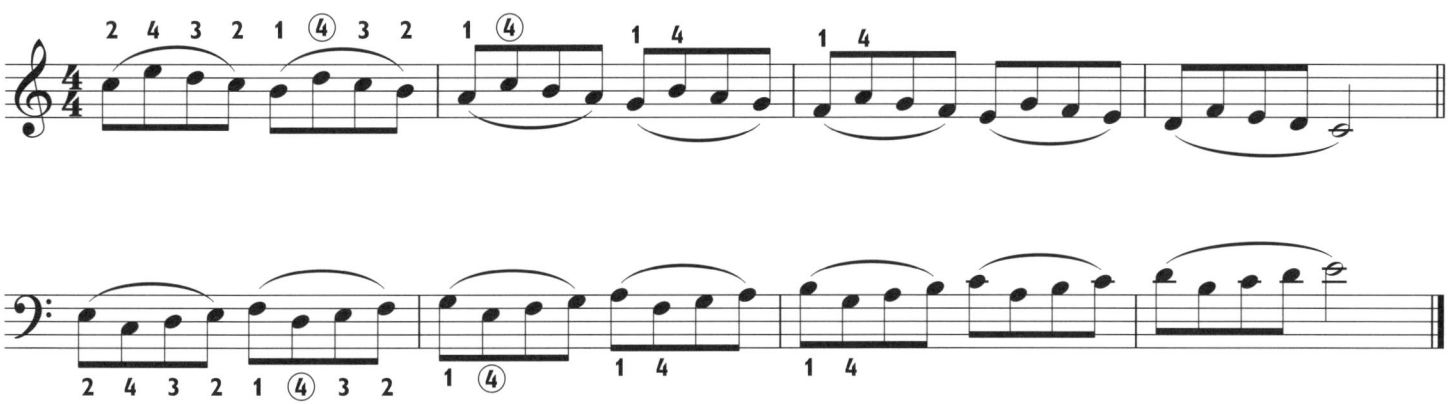

Espressivo

Exercises can sound very boring if you don't move your wrist! Play this expressively with an **Up-and-over** movement each time you play the fifth finger. The movement will help your fifth finger play more firmly and create a slight *crescendo*.

Now try with the left hand:

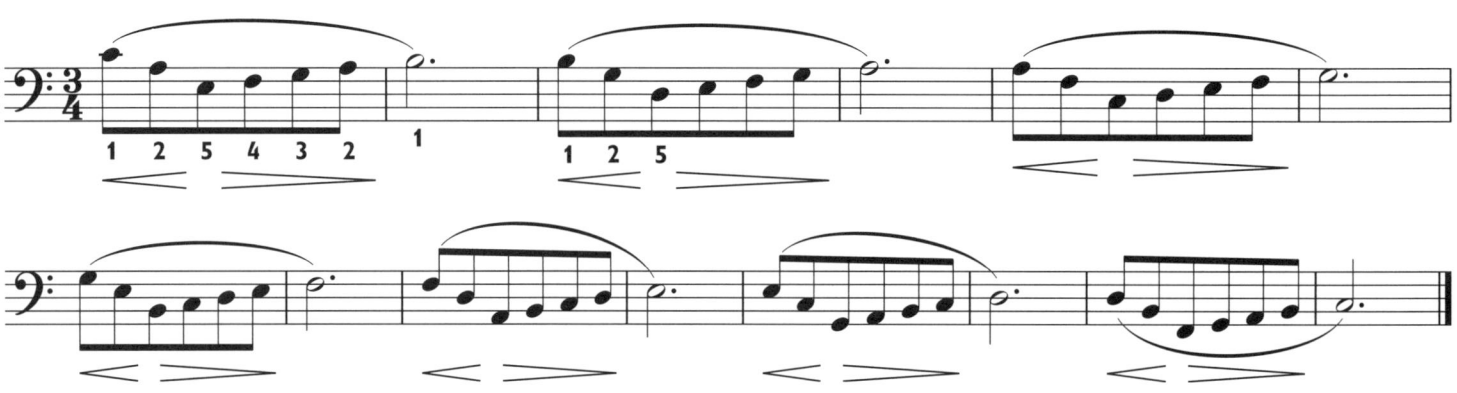

For a bit of fun, try this exercise in a continuing motion, starting slow and gradually getting faster and faster. You can keep going all the way to the end of the keyboard.

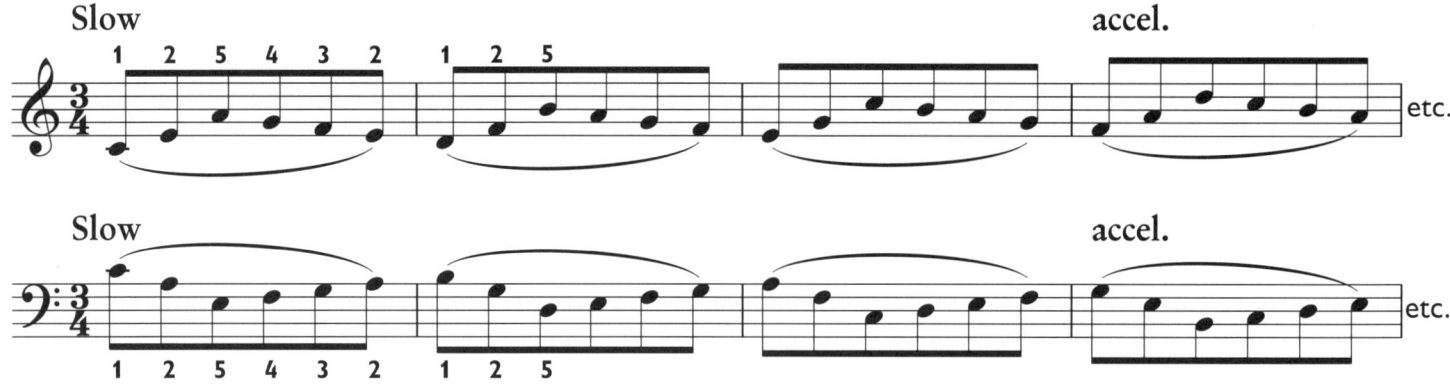

Write in your own dynamics for this exercise. By now, your hands might start to draw circles so naturally you don't even have to think about it.

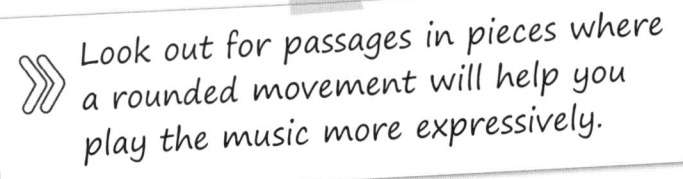

Look out for passages in pieces where a rounded movement will help you play the music more expressively.

Gigue

- Practise hands separately until you can play each hand confidently and gracefully, then play hands together.
- Can you add some interesting dynamics to this piece?

Samuel Arnold

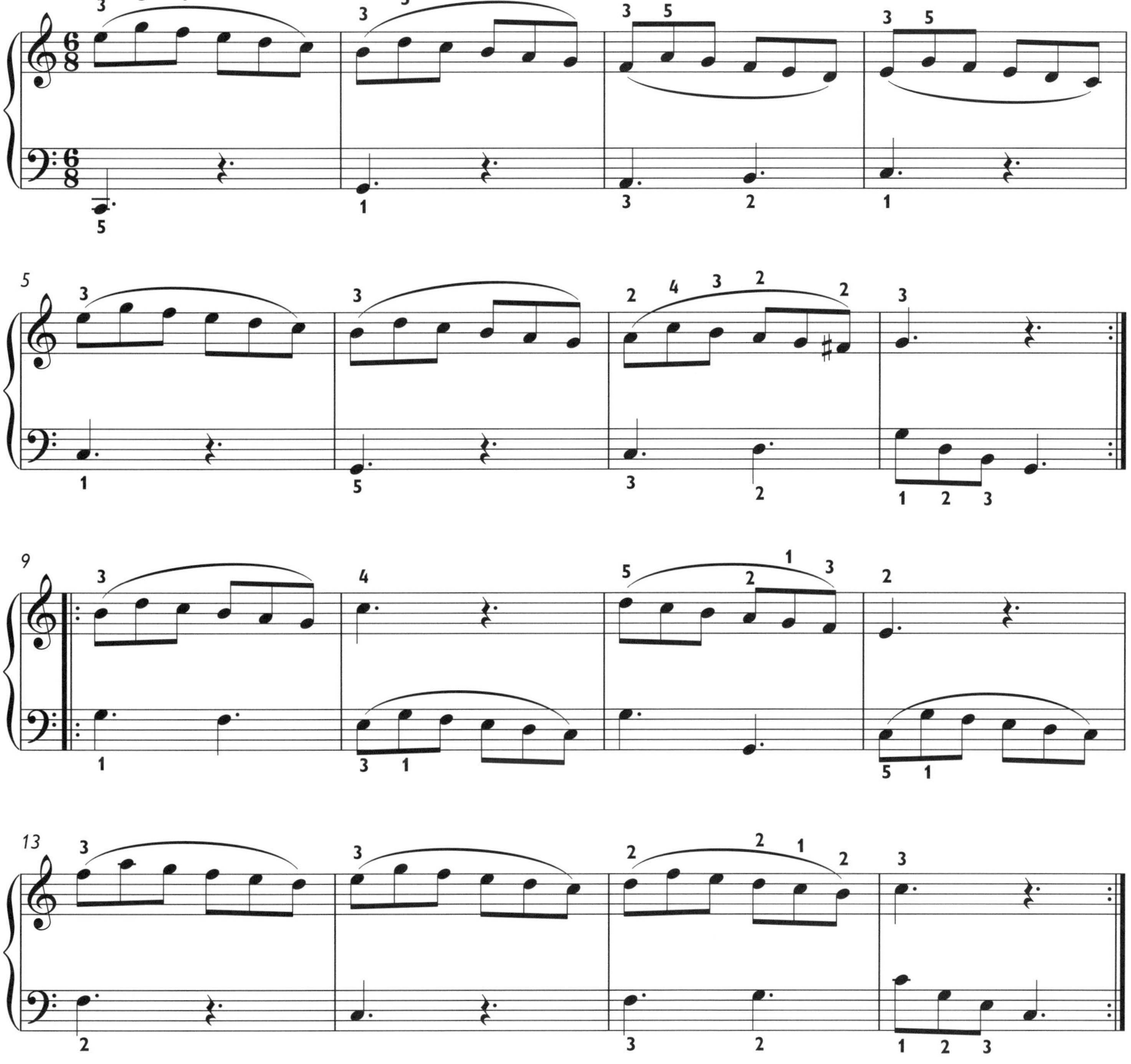

You might also like:

Heinrich Wohlfahrt: 'Patterns', (No. 10) from *Kinder-Klavierschule*
Cornelius Gurlitt: Op. 82 No. 53

Thumb on a black note

Some pentascales start on black notes, so you will need to play the black note with your thumb or fifth finger, but this needn't be awkward!

B♭ major hand position

Help your thumb play the black notes comfortably by moving your hand forward and slotting your second and third fingers in between the black notes to play C and D.

Let's try this B♭ major pentascale in the **Basic five-finger pattern** with the left hand starting on the fifth finger. Like the right hand, if you move your whole hand forward you won't need to curl your third and fourth fingers – they can just play between the black notes:

Now work out the notes for the **Basic five-finger pattern** in E♭ major, A♭ major, D♭ major and G♭ major and play them in each hand.

Whimsy

Aaron Burrows

Sound explorer

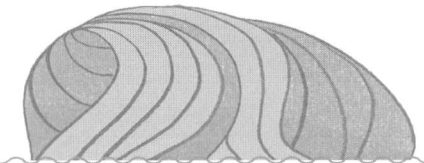

Play a very low note on your keyboard. Listen to the sound die away and only lift your finger when you can no longer hear the sound.

Then do the same with a high note.

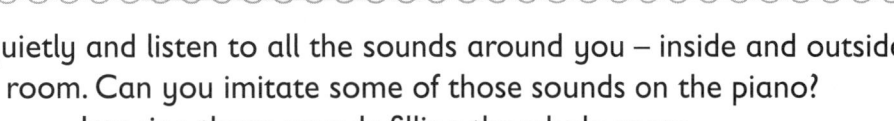

Now sit quietly and listen to all the sounds around you – inside and outside the room. Can you imitate some of those sounds on the piano? Imagine those sounds filling the whole room.

Alternating your hands, touch a flat surface silently with a relaxed hand (a 'mitten hand'). Gradually increase the sound to *forte*, then *diminuendo*.

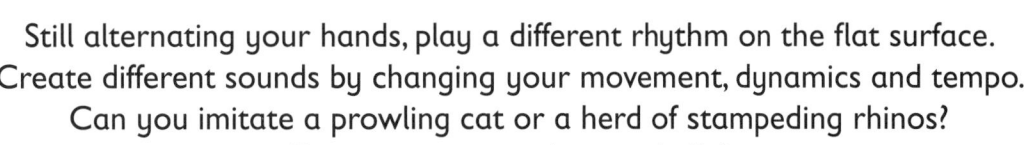

Still alternating your hands, play a different rhythm on the flat surface. Create different sounds by changing your movement, dynamics and tempo. Can you imitate a prowling cat or a herd of stampeding rhinos? Pattering rain or clanging bells?

What can you do to make the piano sound spiky, angry, warm, misty…?

Try creating some of these sounds on the piano. Can you join some of the sounds together to create a story? Don't forget to include some silence!

Matching hands

When the two hands share a melody they need to be able to take over from each other smoothly. In this section, we'll practise how to match our hands so they can share a melody seamlessly.

Equal repetitions

Start by repeating one note, alternating between the right hand and left hand. Does the note sound the same when played by either hand? Then add a *crescendo* and *diminuendo*:

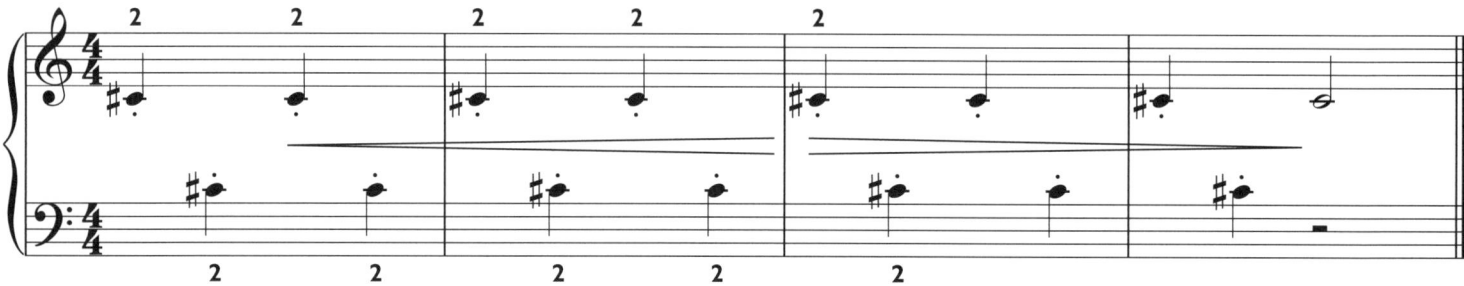

Walking thumbs

On your knee, alternate tapping your right and left thumb. Feel each thumb taking over from the other very smoothly (*legato*). Then walk smoothly from C♯ to D♯ on the keyboard, alternating your right and left thumbs:

Listening and feeling are important parts of technique. Listen carefully to check that all the notes are played *legato*. Do both thumbs feel equal? Repeat with your second fingers and try out some different dynamics.

Smooth take-overs

Now play a *legato* scale on the piano alternating your right and left hands. Make sure that all the notes are played *legato* with the same dynamic – no notes should stick out.

Then play this scale with a gradual *crescendo* and *diminuendo*.

Matching slurs

As you add in more fingers in the next exercises, enjoy the feeling of your hands taking over from each other.

Hickory Dickory Dock

Share this well-known melody between your hands. The left hand plays all the notes with stems pointing downwards and the right hand plays the notes with the stems pointing upwards.

Does every note sound even and *legato*?

Scale flourishes

Now practise sharing these scale flourishes between the hands.

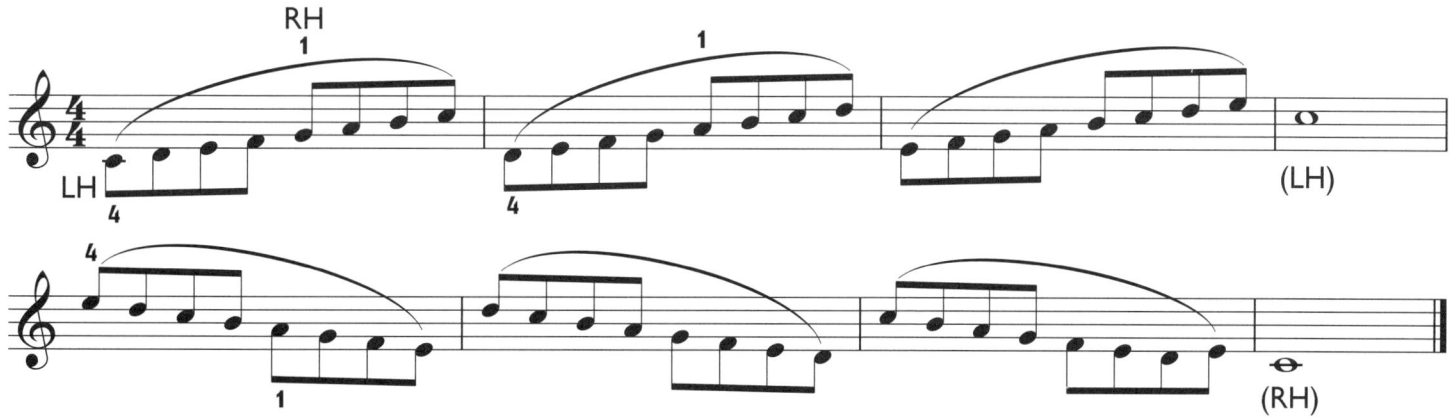

Sliding on the Ice

 Stay close to the keys to avoid any bumps.

Amy Beach
arr. Penelope Roskell

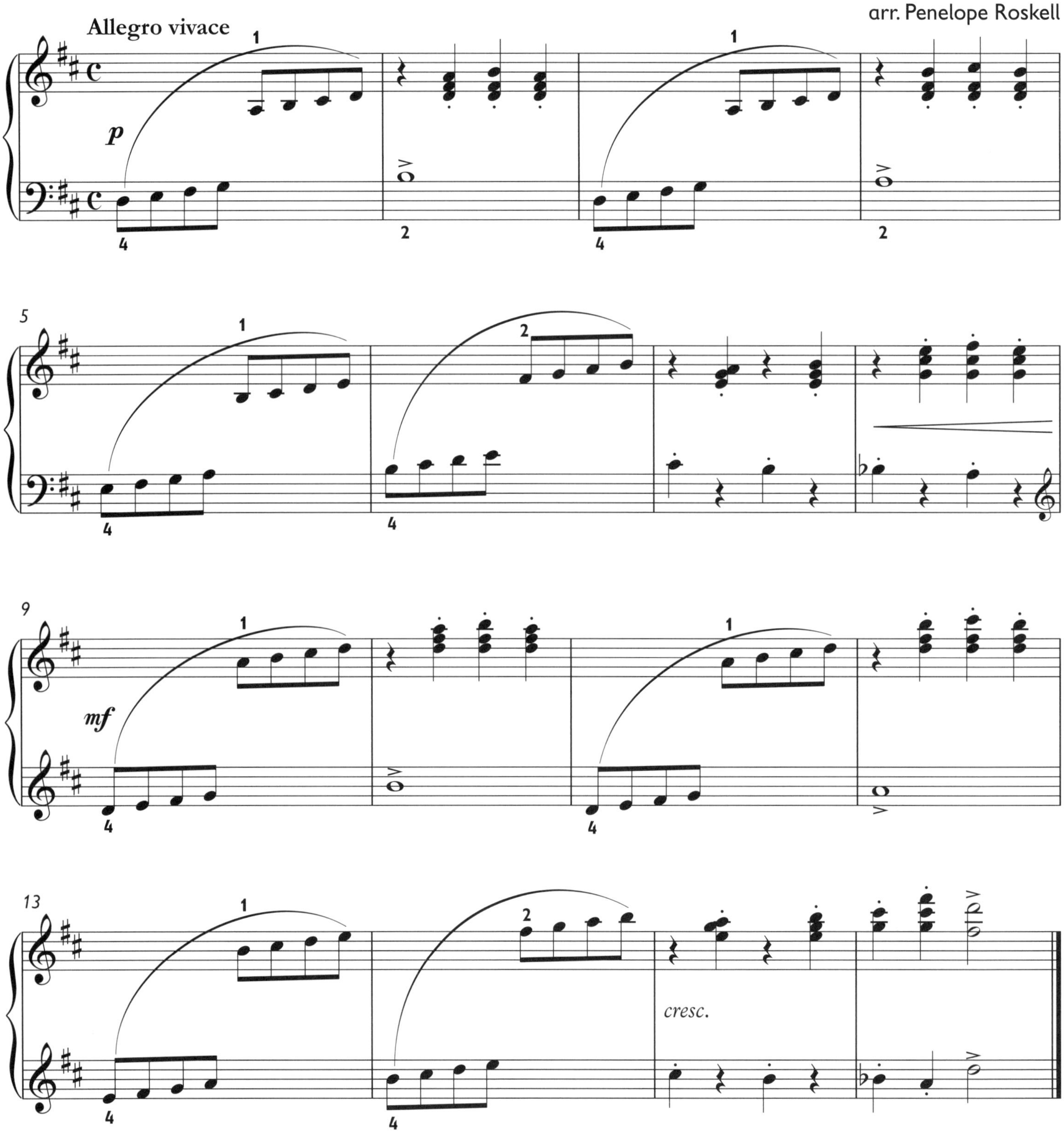

You might also like:

Chee-Hwa Tan: 'The Wind' from *A Child's Garden of Verses*
Marjorie Helyer: 'Dragonflies'

Legato-staccato

In the next two chapters you will practise playing *legato* in one hand and *non-legato* in the other.

Drawing rainbows
Rub your tummy with one hand while you pat your head with the other. Then swap hands. Next, draw big rainbows with one hand while you pat your head with the other. Swap hands.

Stroking the cat
Gently stroke an imaginary cat with one hand then knock on a door loudly with your other hand. Swap hands then try doing both these actions at the same time!

Legato and staccato

Now try slurring the right hand in pairs:

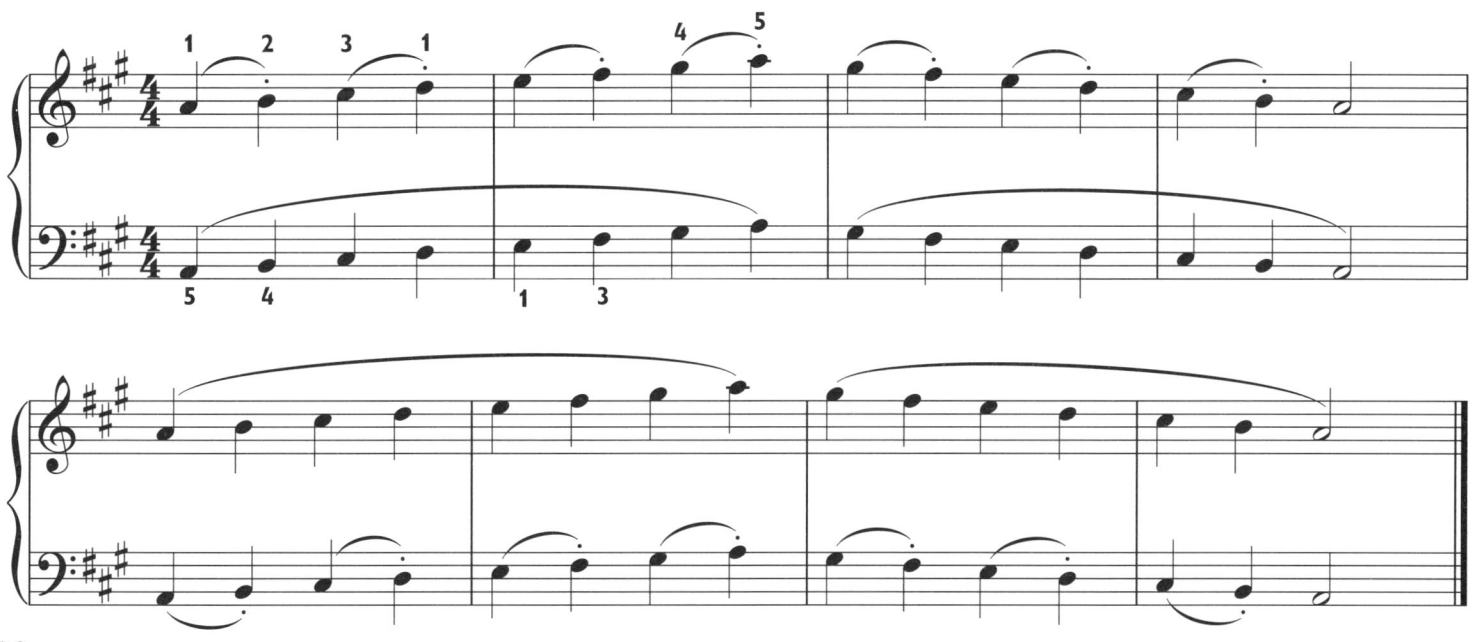

>> Make up your own exercises playing *legato* in one hand and *staccato* in the other.

Frère Jacques

Many pieces include *legato* in one hand and *staccato* in the other. A *canon* is a copycat piece. One voice starts and another follows, copying the melody exactly.

One of the most famous canons is *Frère Jacques*, which you probably recognise!

Start by singing *Frère Jacques* with friends or with your teacher.

Hands separately

Then play voice 1 (the melody in the treble clef) boldly with your right hand while your teacher follows quietly in the bass. Practise the right hand until your hand remembers the notes, the fingering and the articulation (slurs and *legato* or *staccato* markings) automatically – this is called *muscle memory*.

Now do the same playing voice 1 with your left hand.

Hands together

Bars 7 and 8 have *legato* against *staccato*. Practise these bars first. Play the right-hand *staccato* notes with a big swinging motion so they sound like bells. Repeat this until it feels easy.

Then go back to the beginning and practise *Frère Jacques* hands together, two bars at a time, until you can play the whole canon.

Canons are exercises for your ears and your mind as well as for your fingers – try to listen to both parts as you play!

> Listen to the third movement of Gustav Mahler's magnificent first symphony. He included the Frère Jacques theme, played in a minor key by different instruments, starting with the double bass.

Stalking the sloth

Here's another exercise for playing *legato* in one hand and **Down-up slurs** in the other:

Listen very carefully to the rests!

Chasing the Sloth

Enjoy playing this canon by Cornelius Gurlitt. Gurlitt called it *The Chase*, but it also sounds nice played slowly, so let's call it *Chasing the Sloth!*

A melody sounds more expressive if you play descending slurs *diminuendo* and rising phrases *crescendo*.

Cornelius Gurlitt

>> You can come back to this piece later and play it a little faster. You might then have to give it a different name!

You might also like:

Vincent Ho: 'Monkey See, Monkey Do'
Sergei Bortkiewicz: 'Through the Desert'

Calypso

This piece combines *legato* and *staccato* in a syncopated rhythm.

Aaron Burrows

Left-hand melodies

In some pieces, the left hand plays a more interesting melody than the right hand!

Listening challenge

Listen to a recording of one of your favourite pieces – this could be a piano piece, or perhaps a piece that includes a cello, bassoon, trombone, double bass or bass guitar. Can you hear the bass notes clearly?

Now listen to your teacher play *In the Garden* by Gurlitt (p. 32). Try to listen to the bass line all the way through.

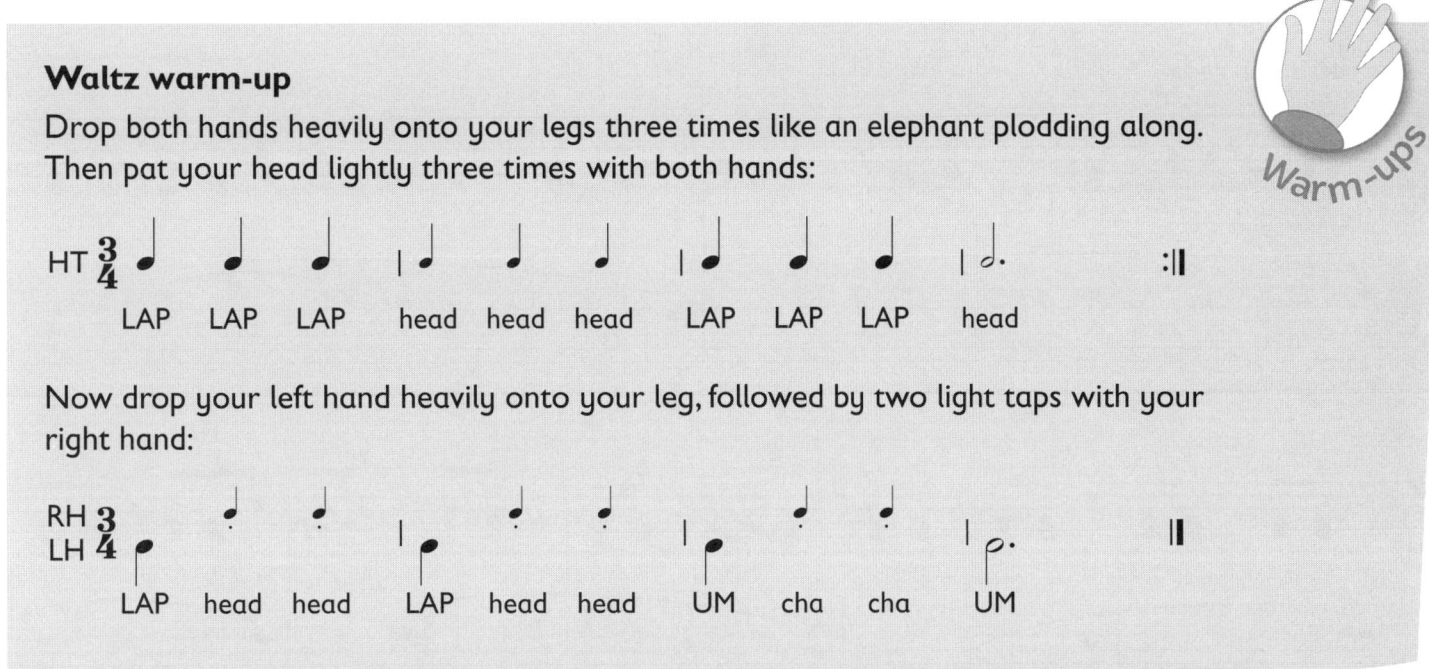

Um cha cha

A waltz is a dance with a strong first beat, followed by two light beats. Practise the first bar of *Um cha cha* until it sounds like an elegant dance. Then play the whole exercise.

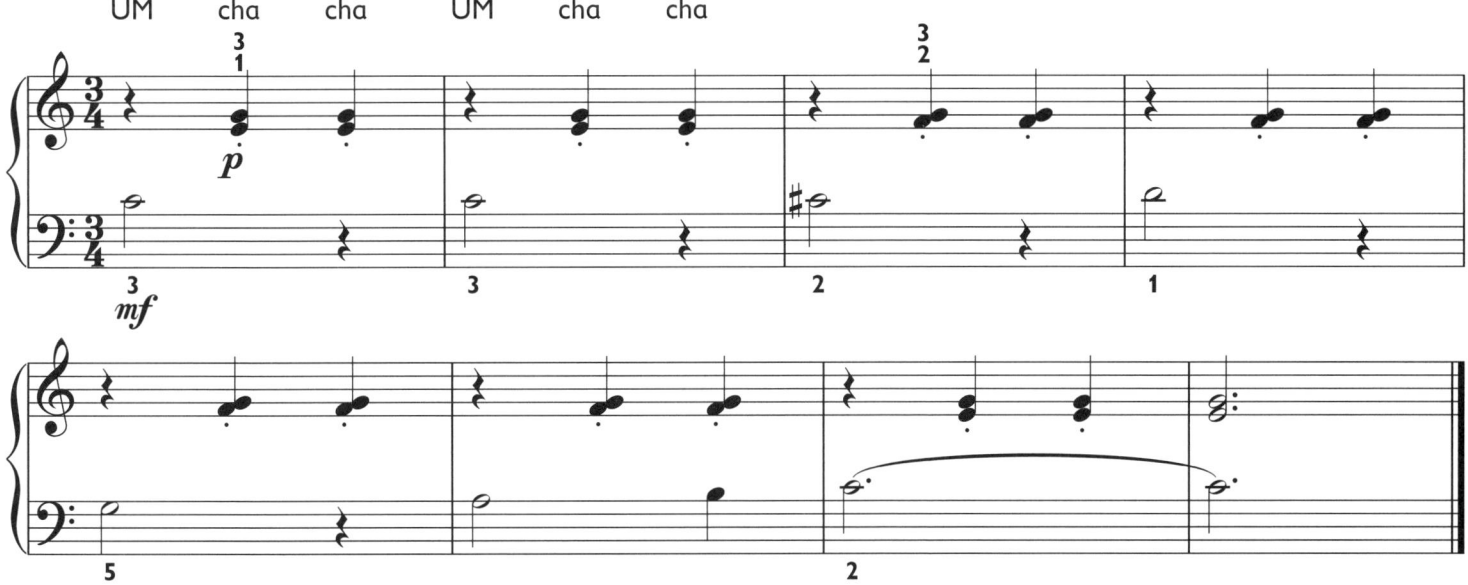

In the Garden

practice pointer

- Practise the left-hand melody on its own before playing hands together. Listen carefully to the melody in the bass as you play this piece.

Cornelius Gurlitt
arr. Penelope Roskell

Allegretto

marcato il canto

You might also like:

William Gillock: 'Little Flower Girl of Paris' and 'The Glass Slipper'

New major scales

Each scale has its own unique pattern of white and black notes but they all share the same sequence of tones and semitones. Each time you learn a new scale, practise it until you can remember how it *looks* and *feels* under your fingers. You will then find that scale much easier to play whenever you find it in a piece of music.

C major scale

Play the C major scale, saying aloud the tones and semitones until you can remember the pattern.

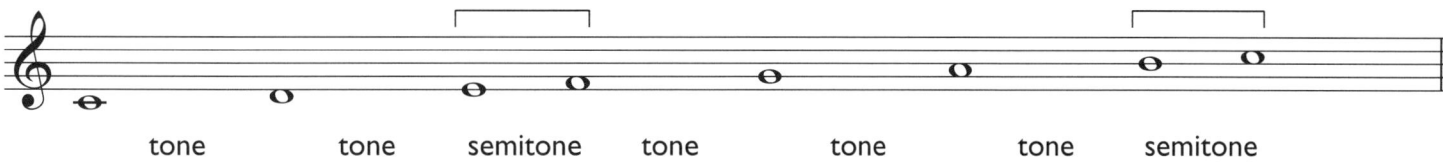

Use the same pattern of tones and semitones to work out the notes for G major, D major and A major.

Right-hand scales

Play the G major scale with your right hand, starting with your thumb, repeating it until you can play it with your eyes closed. Then do the same with D major and A major.

Complete the chart below when you have learnt each scale:

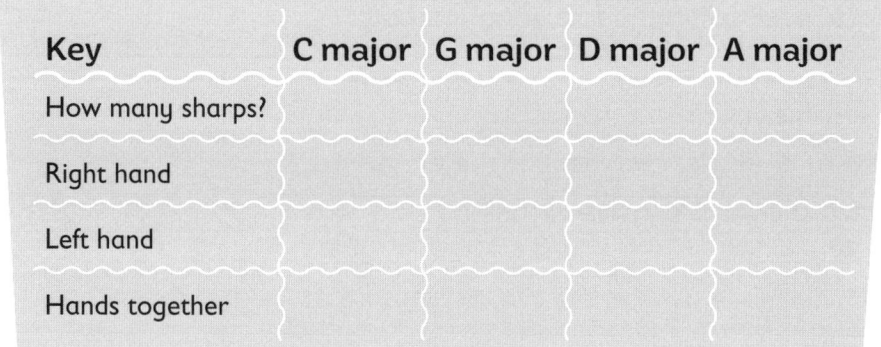

Technique Tip

✔ Place your hand a little nearer to any black notes so you don't have to stretch out your fingers to reach them.

Left-hand scales

Fingering is an important aspect of technique. Good fingering will help you play comfortably, evenly and smoothly.

Not all left-hand scales start with the fifth finger. For instance, D major feels more comfortable and sounds smoother if you start on the second finger.

An easy way to remember this fingering is: fourth and third fingers are long, so they play black notes!

Now play a two-octave scale ascending and descending, starting on 2.

Practise this fingering until you can do it without thinking.

- Say the numbers in circles out loud – this will help you to remember the fingering.

Play the A major scale with the left hand, which also starts with the second finger. The third and fourth fingers play black notes here too.

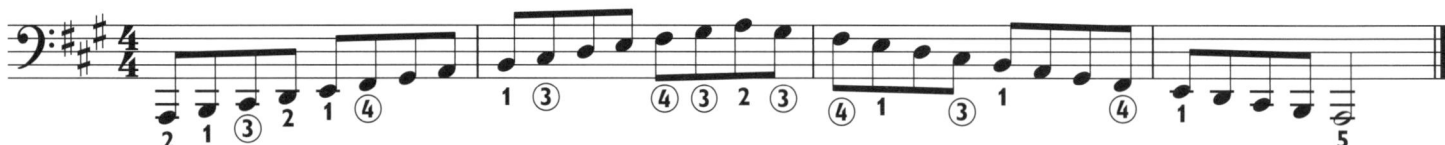

Aim to practise a different scale each week using the following method:
- Work out the scale's key signature.
- Look at the pattern of black and white notes on the piano.
- Practise hands separately ten times until you can't forget the fingering.
- Start to play hands together, using the **Add-a-note** technique you learnt in Level 1.
- Gradually increase the tempo.

 Practise the E major scale hands separately and hands together and revise the F major scale from Level 1 (page 30-34).

Expressive scales

Don't let your scales sound boring! Each time you practise a scale, treat it like a beautiful melody. Remember, good fingering will help you play scales evenly, and flowing arm movements will make your scales sound smooth and elegant.

Stroking the cat

Stroke an imaginary cat or dog in front of you. You can use the same stroking motion to play an expressive scale on the piano.

Skipping-rope technique

This technique will help you smooth out any bumps in your scales. Hold down your third finger on a table and let your arm hang freely like a rope. Then swing your arm loosely from side to side to help your thumb pass under.

Flow sideways

Now let's use the **Skipping-rope technique** at the piano with the scale of D major. Swing your right hand thumb under F♯ and back again:

Smooth scales

Now play a D major scale using the **Add-a-note** technique. **Stroke the cat** a little more each time you add a note, so your arm flows smoothly sideways.

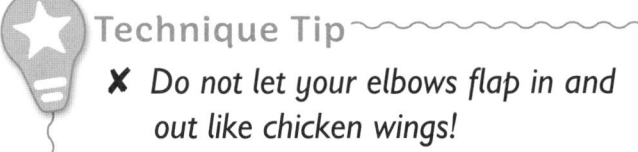

Technique Tip
✗ *Do not let your elbows flap in and out like chicken wings!*

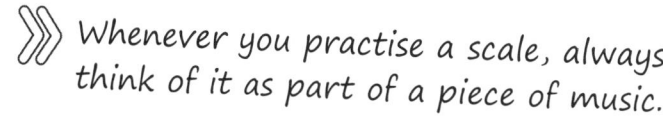

》 Whenever you practise a scale, always think of it as part of a piece of music.

Shapely scales

Keep repeating the following exercise until you feel your hand naturally drawing a rounded shape as it ascends and descends the scale.

Look at the patterns in the next piece. You may recognise it – it starts with part of a famous sonata by Mozart. Feel the expressive gestures of your hand as it flows along the keyboard. Add some dynamic markings – remember that a slight *crescendo* and *diminuendo* gives a scale shape.

Mini-Mozart

 Record yourself playing this and listen to the recording. Does the scale sound expressive? Try playing scales with your eyes closed. Use your ears, not your eyes!

W.A. Mozart
arr. Penelope Roskell

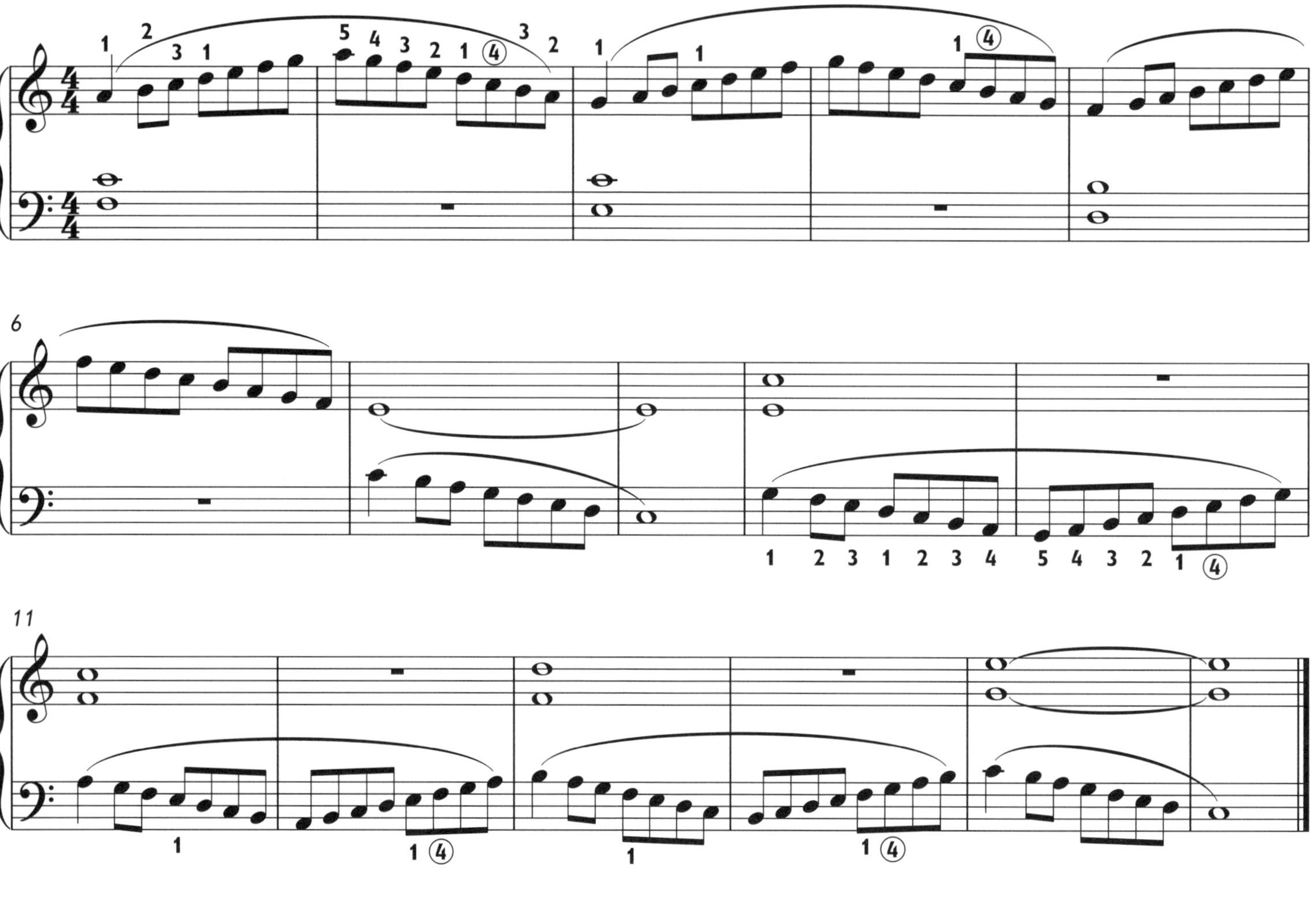

Daydream

Aaron Burrows

Alberti bass

The *Alberti bass* is a type of bass line named after composer Domenico Alberti who included it in many of his compositions. Many other Classical composers, such as Mozart, Haydn and Clementi also used the *Alberti bass* in their pieces.

An *Alberti bass* can be played fast or slow and the notes are played in this order:

Let's first revise the arm rotation we use for the *Alberti bass*:

Slow warm-up: The rolling ship
Imagine you are in a ship which is rolling from side to side with the waves. Place your hand on your leg and rotate your arm to rock from thumb to fifth finger. Then rock slowly from thumb to third finger.

Fast warm-up: Flip flop spider
On a flat surface, keep your arm very relaxed as you flip your hand all the way over and back again. Then make much smaller movements as you rotate quite quickly between your thumb and fifth finger.

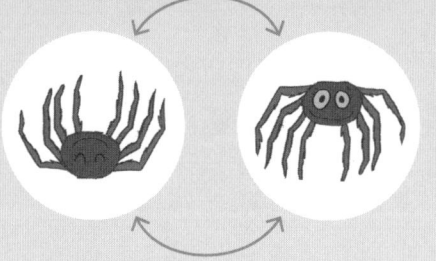

Alberti bass technique

Now at the piano, rotate from finger 5 to 1. Then rotate from 3 to 1 – you will find you hardly need to rotate at all for this. Combine these in the next exercise. Play slowly at first, then try it a little faster:

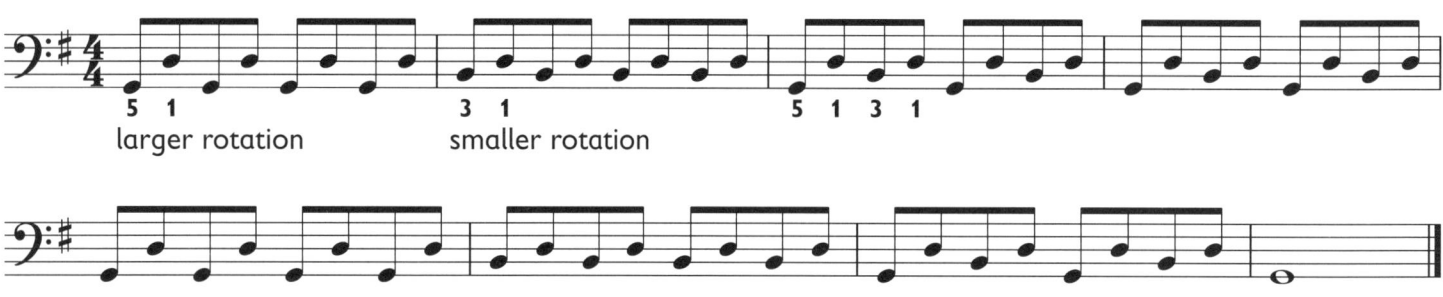

Technique Tips
- ✗ Don't rotate so far that your hand rolls over onto its side!
- ✓ Play on the thumb corner and keep your fifth finger nicely rounded.

Preparing the accompaniment

It's helpful to think of an *Alberti bass* as a broken-up chord rather than as individual notes. Play the notes as block chords first, then break them up:

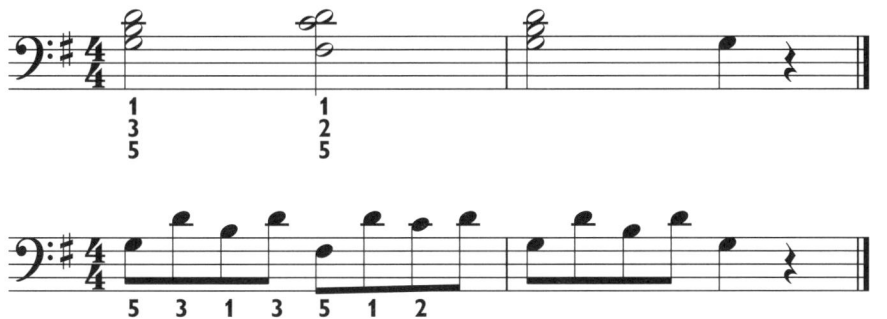

> Can you make up some different patterns containing the notes G, B and D, perhaps in ¾ time?

You will find this *Alberti bass* pattern in the extract from Thomas Attwood's *Sonatine* below.

Sonatine (extract)

> Find a piece with chords in the left hand and play these as an Alberti bass.

You might also like:

Thomas Attwood: Sonatine in G (complete)
Thomas Attwood: Allegro in C
Carl Czerny: Op. 599 No. 36

Broken thirds

You can now use the rolling rotation action from the *Alberti bass* to play broken thirds using three different fingerings.

Rolling along

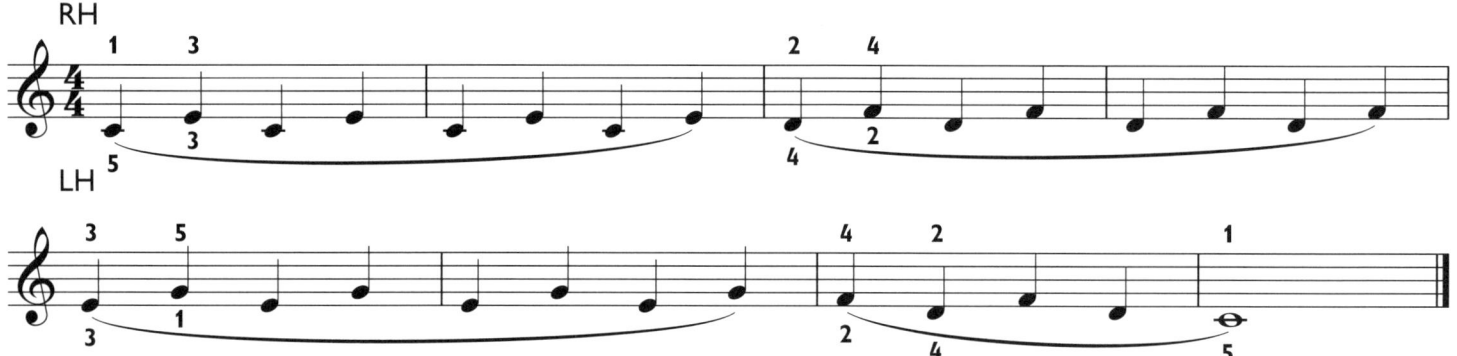

Play the left hand one octave lower.

Wriggling up the scale

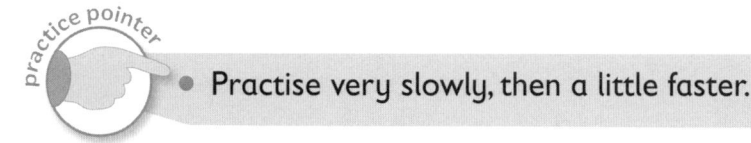

practice pointer • Practise very slowly, then a little faster.

Thirdly

Allegro moderato

Aaron Burrows

Harmonic minor scales

The *natural minor scale* of A minor, which you learnt in Primer B, has only white notes like its relative major key, C major:

If you raise the seventh note one semitone, it turns into a *harmonic minor scale*.

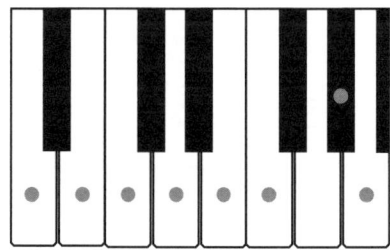

A harmonic minor scale

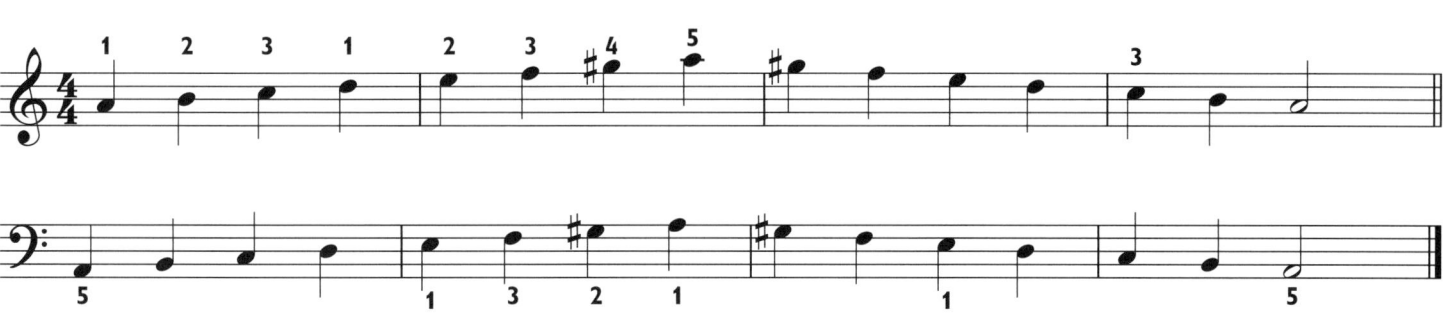

Harmonic minor scales can sound:

Creepy

Mournful

Exotic

 With the help of your teacher, work out the notes for these harmonic minor scales:

D minor   G minor   C minor

 **Technique Tips**
- ✔ Keep your arm flowing all the way up to the top note — this will help you reach the G♯ more comfortably.
- ✔ Place your hand forward a little so you can reach the black notes easily.
- ✔ Remember to play the thumb on its corner.

Key	D minor	G minor	C minor
How many flats?			
Raised note			
Learnt (✔)			

Waltz

The elbow spa

Your elbows don't need to work hard at the piano – they just hang floppily most of the time! When your elbows are relaxed, you will find that many techniques, especially arpeggios, become easier and sound more flowing as well. So let's take your elbows to the spa!

Elbow warm-ups

~ Stand up and shake your arms.

~ Swing your arms forward and back, keeping your elbows very relaxed.

~ At the piano, skim your arms to opposite ends of the keyboard and back. Feel your elbows open and close – do they feel elasticky?

~ Skim both arms along the surface of the keys towards the highest notes, then towards the lowest notes.

~ Rest your hand in a sleepy spider position (see page 16). Can you wiggle your fingers while your arms stay soft and floppy?

Elbows at the piano

~ Play a harmonic minor scale with floppy relaxed elbows. Don't flap your elbows like chicken wings!

~ Play your favourite melody, keeping your shoulders and elbows relaxed.

~ Parachute gently onto a chord. Check that your elbow stays relaxed as you land but keep your hand in its naturally rounded position.

~ Parachute heavily onto a chord with elephant steps. Can you keep your elbow relaxed?

Keep reminding yourself to keep your elbows soft and floppy when you practise!

One-octave arpeggios

An arpeggio is like an extended broken chord. It is made up of the first, third, fifth and eighth notes of the scale.

Sing the sol-fa names of the notes as you play the C major scale and arpeggio.

Detached arpeggios

Play the C major arpeggio *detached*, with a light bobbing movement on each note. Then play all of these arpeggios detached:

- D minor
- E minor
- F major
- G major
- A minor

They are all white-note arpeggios so they all feel the same. You will be able to learn them all very quickly!

Now play the D major arpeggio detached:

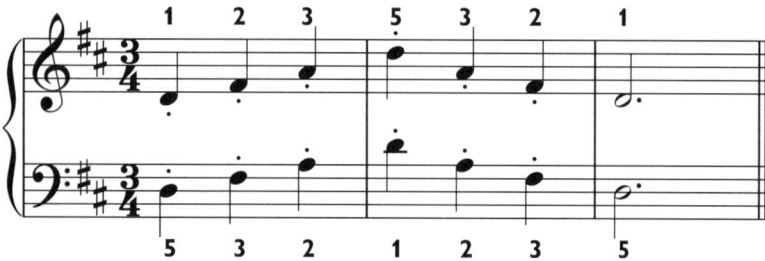

Then play major arpeggios starting on A and E.

Legato arpeggios

To play arpeggios *legato*, your wrist needs to swing sideways to help the fingers reach their notes.

Swinging wrists

Rest your second finger lightly on a table and swing your wrist from side to side. Enjoy the feeling of freedom in your arm as it swings and remember to keep your elbow relaxed.

Practising *legato* arpeggios

Play the following exercises for the right and left hands *legato*.

 **Technique Tips**

✔ Swivel your wrist from side to side in each bar to help your fingers reach their notes.
✘ You don't need to stretch out your fingers – your wrist can do the work for you!
✔ Swing your wrist and arm a little further in bars 5–6.
✘ No chicken wings! Keep your elbows floppy.

 Can you play bars 5 and 6 comfortably?

Yes
Play all the arpeggios you practised earlier *legato*, hands separately then hands together.

No
Continue to play arpeggios slightly detached until your hand is larger.

Musical arpeggios

How would you play an arpeggio if it was in a piece of music? Try using a rounded movement. Play the ascending notes with a low wrist, then raise your wrist for the descending notes. You could also add a little *crescendo* and *diminuendo*.

- Practise a different one-octave arpeggio each day.
- Keep your fingers light and your arm relaxed.

 Find the notes for the arpeggios of G minor, C minor and F minor and play those.

Look out for arpeggios in other pieces and make sure you play them with a swinging wrist.

As the Wind Cries

Andante (tempo rubato)

Aaron Burrows

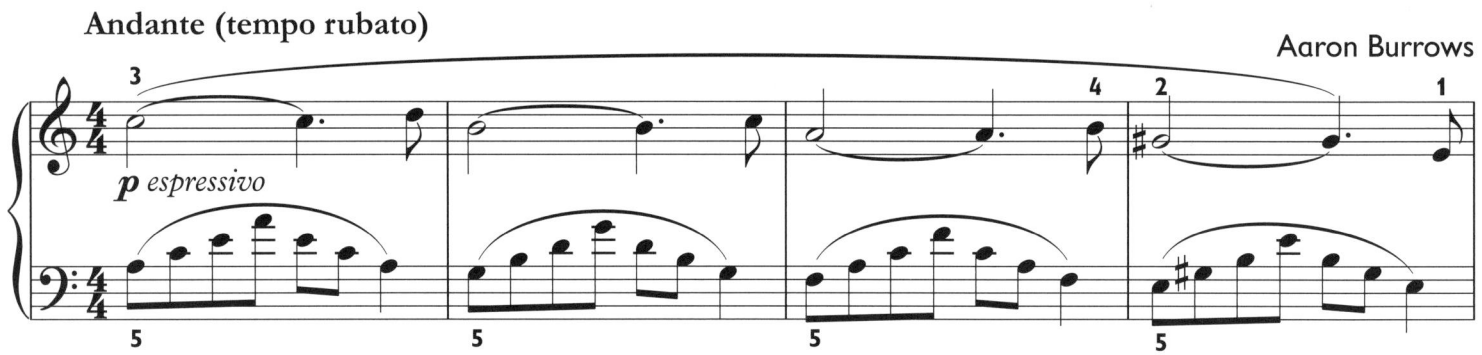

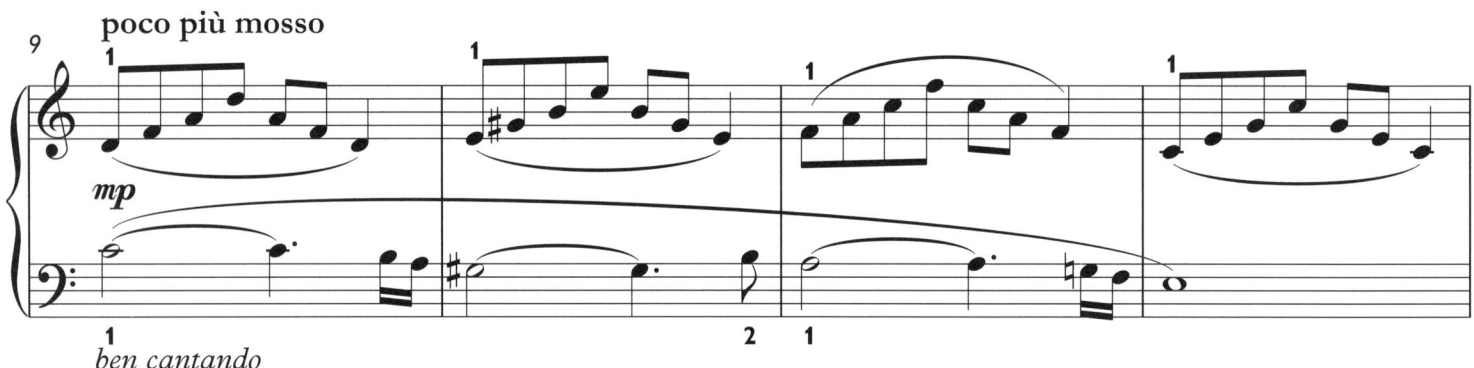

You might also like:

Ludovico Einaudi: 'Song for Gavin'

Jean Louis Streabbog: 'The Orphan' (No. 4) Op. 64

J.S. Bach: 'Minuet in G' BWV Anh. 116

Crossing hands

Swatting flies

Sit at a table and move your hand around quickly as if you are swatting flies! Then at the piano, drop your hand onto clusters of notes. Move quickly between high notes and low notes. It doesn't matter which notes you play – just swat as many flies as quickly as you can! Swat them loudly, then stealthily and repeat with your other hand.

Pinball

Now jump between these notes on the piano, feeling your arm ping lightly from side to side like a pinball:

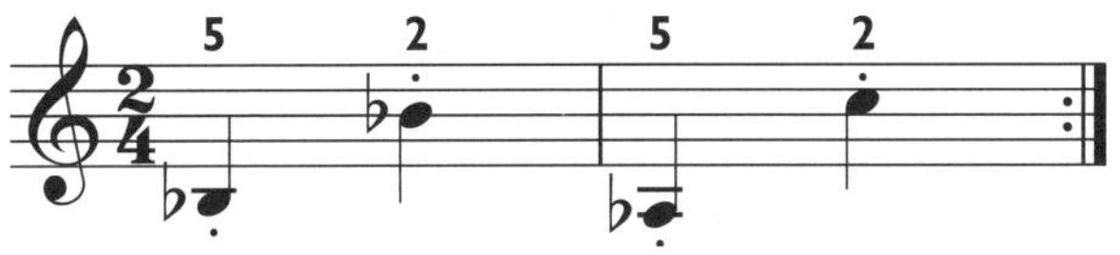

Loading Screen

This piece is easier than it looks! Play the rhythm on a table first, then learn the chords.

- Always watch your left hand as you play this piece.
- Keep your right wrist lower than your left so the left hand can cross over easily.

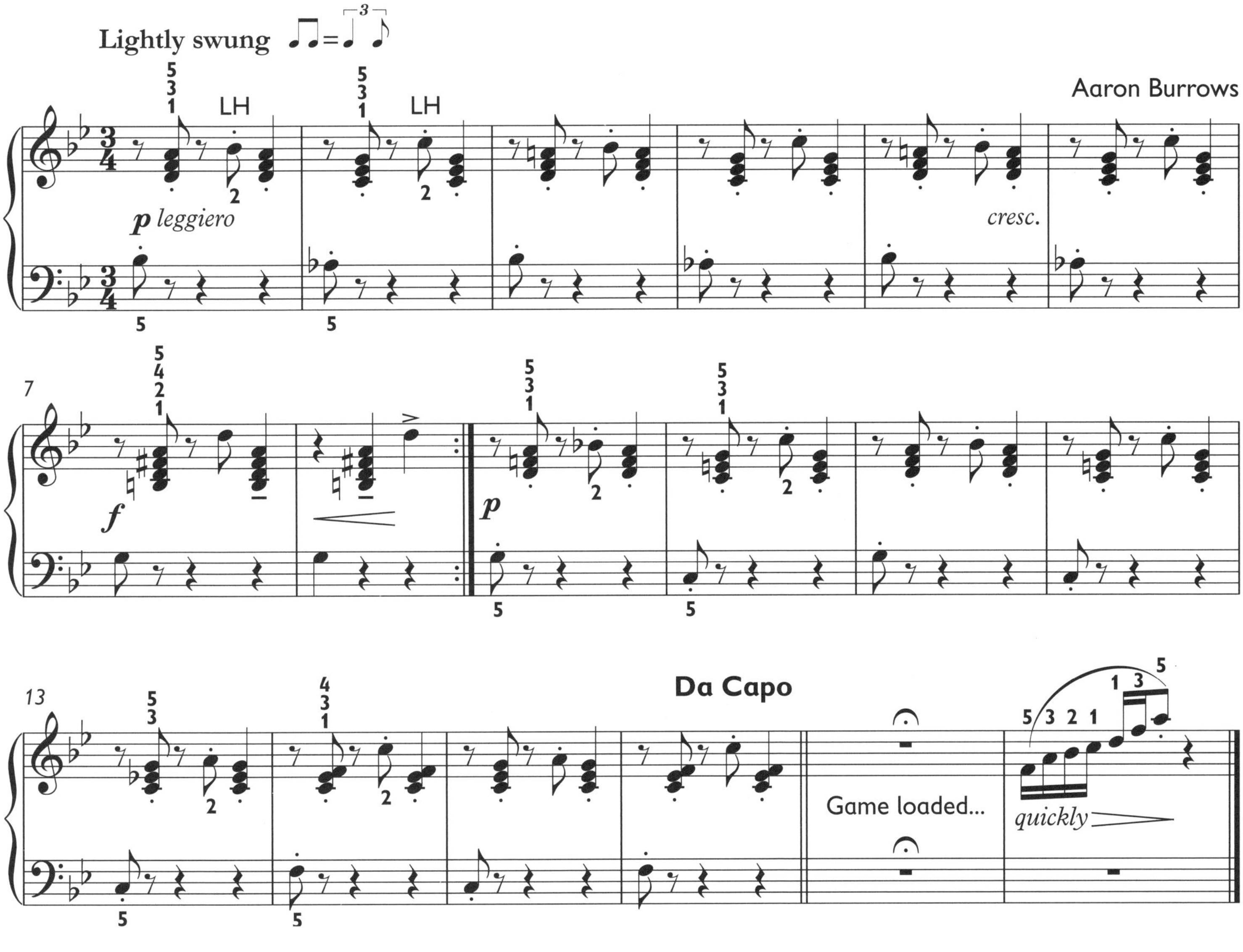

Aaron Burrows

47

Pedal explorer

Sustaining notes

The right pedal is called the *sustaining pedal*. It makes a note continue to sound after your fingers have released the key.

- Press the right pedal down. Play the lowest note on the keyboard *staccato* and count how many seconds it lasts. Then do the same with the highest note and count the seconds until the sound dies away.

What's going on inside the piano?

If you have the opportunity to play an acoustic piano, open it up and have a look inside:

- Press the pedal then release it. What do you see happen?
- Press the pedal and sing or shout loudly across the strings. Then do the same without the pedal. What do you hear?

Joining and combining notes

The pedal also helps us to combine notes and join them together to make interesting sounds. Keep the pedal down as you play each of these:

- a C major scale
- a C major arpeggio
- a chromatic scale in the bass
- a chromatic scale on very high notes
- all of the black notes from low to high

Which of these sounds do you like most?

Alligator jaw
Place your heel on the floor, then flap your toes up and down like an alligator's jaw keeping your heel on the ground. Say 1–2, 1–2, 1–2, aloud as you do this.

Controlling the pedal
Then, sitting at the piano, move your foot onto the right pedal (the sustaining pedal) and press down and up. Keep your heel on the floor and move the pedal quietly, without banging.

Coordinating hands and feet
Can you draw big circles with your arms while you move the pedal up and down with your foot?

Legato pedalling

> The sustaining pedal helps us join notes or chords together *legato*.

First you need to learn to coordinate your foot with your hands (and even count out loud at the same time!).

Press the pedal down, then stay down for two beats, then lift up. Keep repeating this, saying the words out loud until it feels easy.

Up, down, stay down   Up, down, stay down   Up, down, stay down   Up

Legato pedalling

Try playing this scale *legato* with only your third finger. You will need to change the pedal for each note:

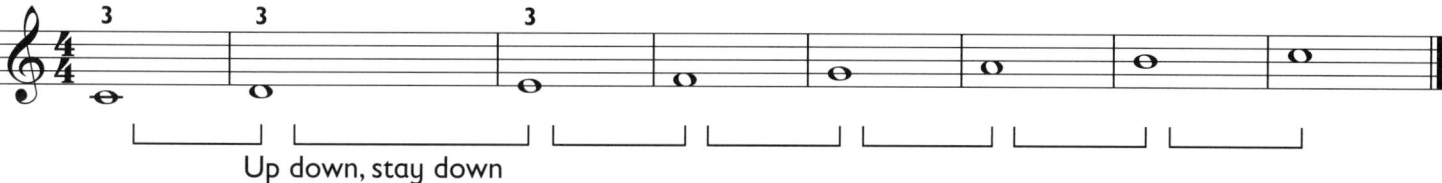

Up down, stay down

Say *up down, stay down* out loud as you play each note.

Now play the scale with your left hand third finger. Instead of saying the words, this time just change the pedal with a neat up-down movement as you play each note.

Listen carefully to check that the pedal is joining all the notes *legato*, without any gaps or overlap between the notes.

This may all seem hard at first, but it gets easier as you get used to it.

It may help to remember that *legato pedalling* is like a see-saw — when your finger goes *down*, your foot comes *up*.

49

Pachelbel's Canon with pedal

Now you can be in charge of the pedal as you play *Pachelbel's Canon* with your teacher. Change the pedal as you play each chord.

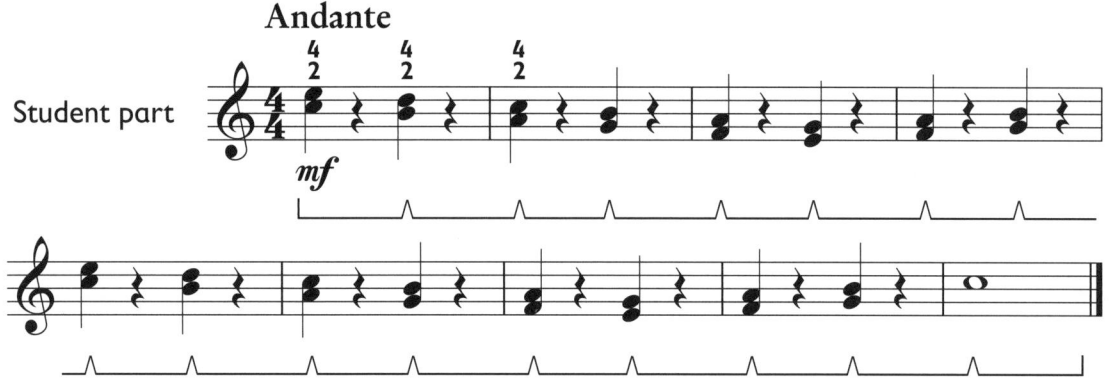

Chord changes

Here you only need to change the pedal when the chord changes. The right hand and left hand are playing the same chords so you only need to change the pedal at the beginning of each bar.

These pieces from Level 1 can all now be played with legato pedalling:
Fanfare (p. 12), *Solemn Procession* (p. 46), *Overture,* (p. 47), *Variation* (p. 52).

50

The Lonely Gondolier

Aaron Burrows

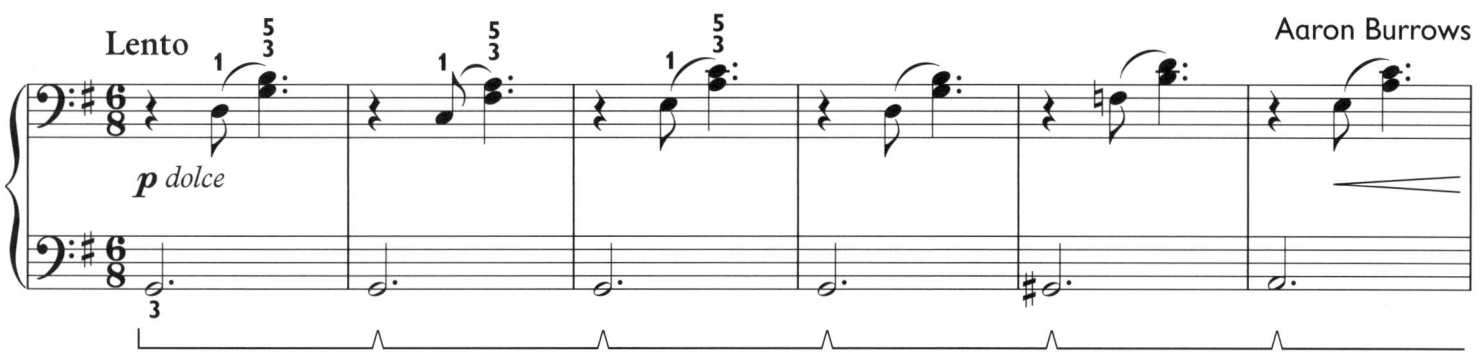

>> Look at some other pieces with your teacher and decide whether they would sound good with legato pedalling.

You might also like:
Anne Crosby Gaudet: 'Angelfish'
Naoko Ikeda: 'Raft of Flowers'
Cornelius Gurlitt: 'Theme' from *Theme and Variation* Op. 228

Combining techniques

Look out for these techniques on the first page of the *Sonatina*.

- Down-up hop
- Broken thirds
- Alberti bass
- C and G major scales
- A one-octave arpeggio
- Rounded movements

Which techniques can you see on the second page?

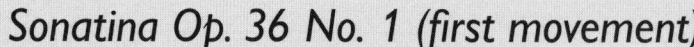

Sonatina Op. 36 No. 1 (first movement)

Muzio Clementi
arr. Penelope Roskell

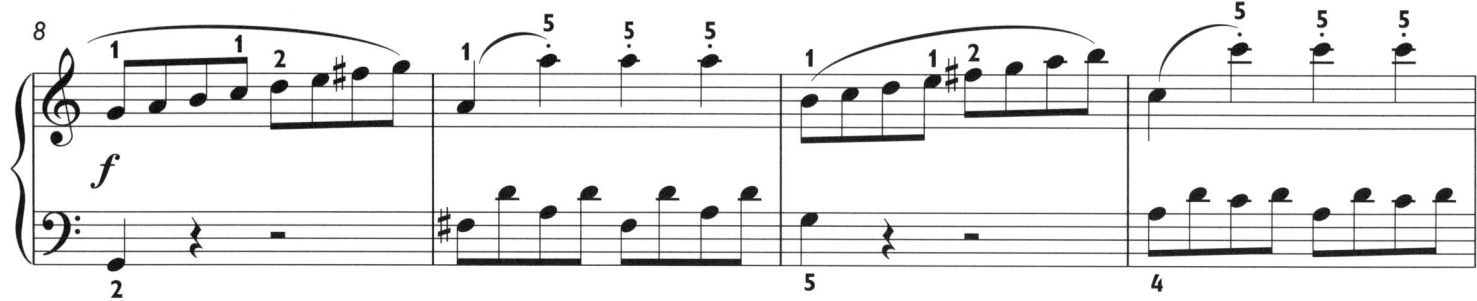
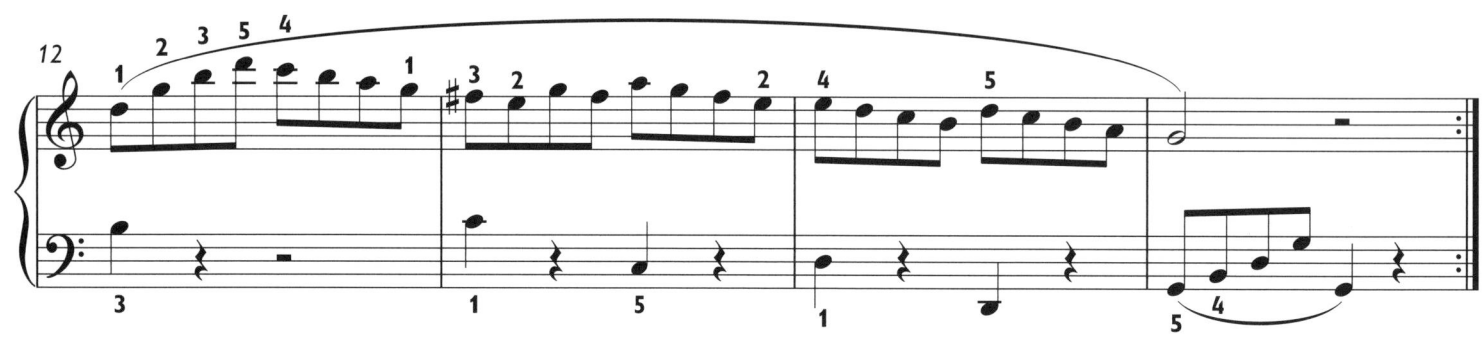

SECONDO

Broadway

Aaron Burrows

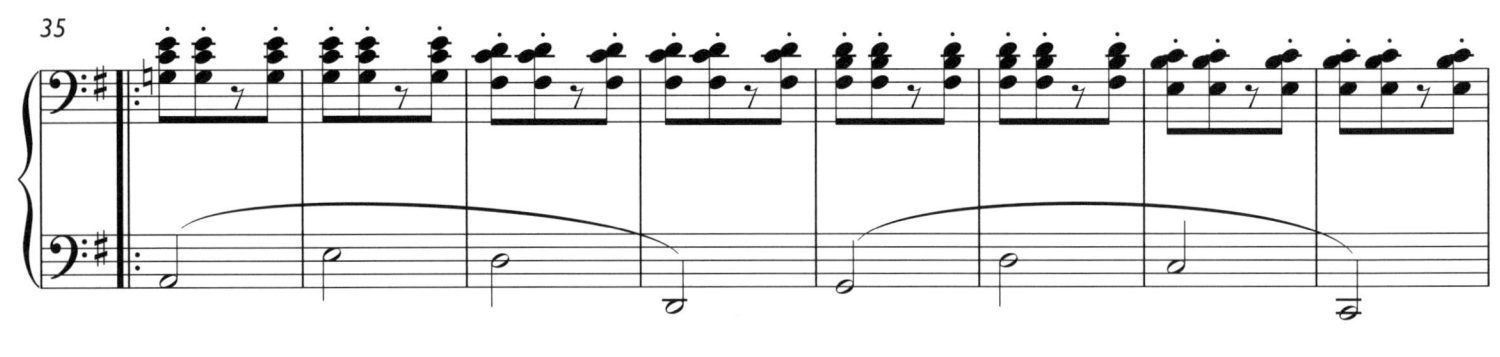

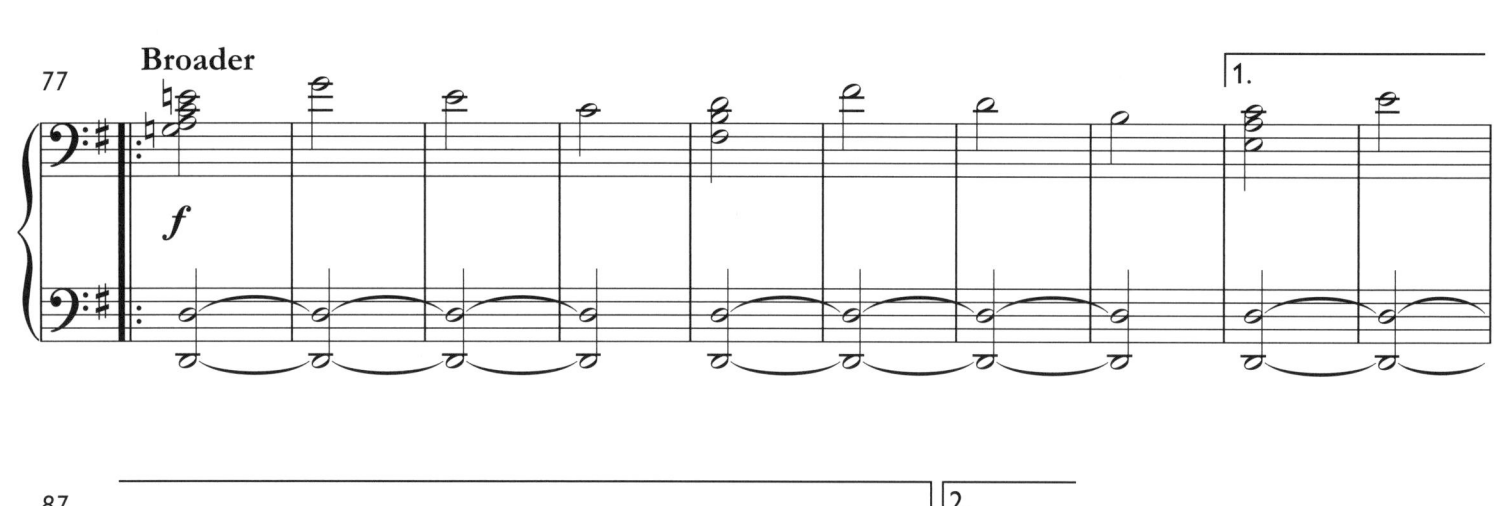
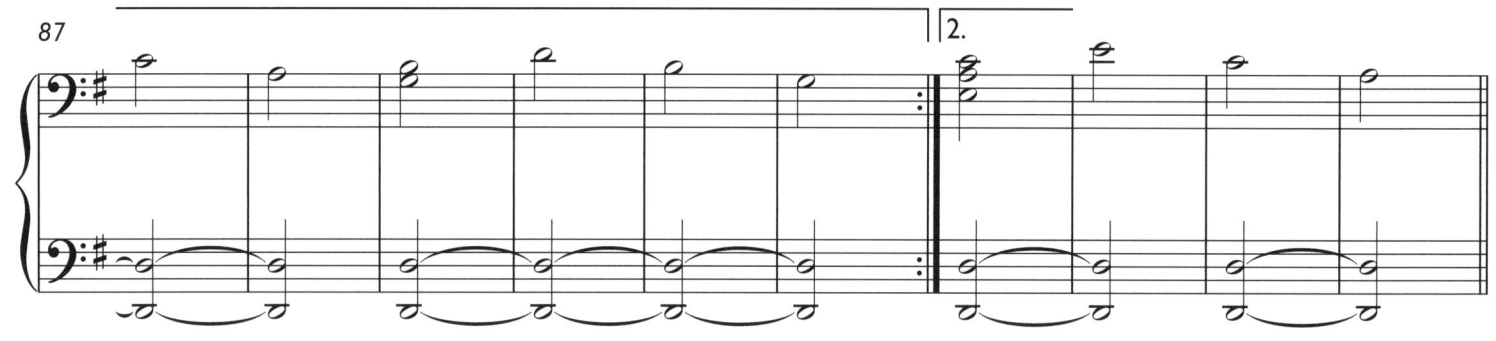

Teaching notes

 Video demonstrations can be accessed via the QR code, or by visiting www.fabermusic.com/ep/essential-piano-technique

R = Revision (especially relevant to those new to this series)

LO = Learning Objectives

TT = Teaching Tips

RP = Related Pieces, either from *Essential Piano Technique*, or other recommended repertoire which is readily available.

Page 6 **Circle warm-ups**

- **LO** To keep the shoulder, elbow and wrist joints supple.
- **TT** Encourage students to warm up regularly before playing.

Page 7 **Sitting posture**

- **LO** To establish a habit of playing with well-balanced posture and good handshape.
- **TT** Allow the student time to adjust the height of the seat at the beginning of each lesson. A simple way to check the distance of the seat from the keyboard is to straighten the elbow and reach the hand forward to touch the fallboard (or equivalent) with the back of the hand.
See also *The Complete Pianist*, pp. 42-48.

Page 8 **Hand positions old and new**

- **R** I've a happy tale to tell (Primer A, p. 26); Flabby tabby cat (Primer B, p. 16); Down-up hop hop (Primer B, p. 20); The parachute touch and Elephant steps (Primer B, pp. 7–11).
- **LO** To become familiar with the hand position for pentascales, broken chords and chords in common keys, keeping a naturally rounded handshape with evenly curved fingers.
- **TT** Repeat the basic five-finger pattern in each new key the student encounters. Some students may like to add first inversion and second inversion chords.
- **RP** Pauline Hall and Paul Drayton: 'The Very Vicious Velociraptor' (Grade 1, Trinity, 2021–23)
Ignatius Sancho: 'Douze de Decembre'
Anton Diabelli: 'The First Twelve Lessons' Op. 123 No. 3
Anon.: 'A Toy' from *Fitzwilliam Virginal Book* (Grade 1, ABRSM, 2021–22).

Page 12 **Circular movements**

- **R** Wavy broken chords (Primer B, p. 25).
- **LO** To play expressively using a rounded (circular, or elliptical) wrist movement. To combine rounded movements.
- **TT** In all these exercises, the left hand moves clockwise and the right hand anticlockwise. Start with large movements, then gradually minimise them. Guard against excessive downward wrist movement – the thumb should still land on its corner.
'Orbit': Familiarise the student with the $\frac{5}{8}$ time signature and explore the changing hand positions before learning the piece. The quavers are played with one circular movement per bar.
- **RP** Franz Behr: 'In May'
Victoria Proudler: 'Rainbow's End' from *Piano Grades are Go!*

Page 15 **Hand gym**

- (R) Hand gym (Primer A, p. 15); Finger gym (Primer B, p. 12); Thumb gym (Primer B, p. 24).
- (LO) To strengthen the finger end (DIP) joints (Itchy leg). To strengthen the intrinsic hand muscles which support the hand arch (Snapping crocodile). To strengthen hypermobile thumbs (Squeezing the circle).
- (TT) Snapping crocodile: Keep the second finger straight. The movement comes from the main knuckle (MCP joint), not from the middle (PIP) joint.
  Tapping at the piano: If the hand and arm are relaxed, a slight forearm rotation will naturally occur each time the thumb taps. See also *The Complete Pianist*, pp. 510-515.

Page 16 **Strengthening the weaker fingers**

- (R) Hand gym (Primer A, p. 15); Finger gym (Primer B, p. 12); Hand gym (Level 2, p. 15).
- (LO) To strengthen the intrinsic hand muscles and develop independent finger action and a strong hand arch.
- (TT) Never force the weaker fingers. Remind students to practise these exercises little and often, ideally for a month or more. Keep the arm and wrist relaxed. Don't be concerned if the fifth finger moves in conjunction with the fourth and vice versa – just the *intention* to move one finger is adequate training at this stage.

Page 17 **Playing with 4 and 5**

- (R) Drop and walk (Primer B, p. 13); Strengthening the weaker fingers (Level 2, p. 16); Circular movements (Level 2, p. 12).
- (LO) To develop confidence in playing with the weaker fingers. Combines finger strength with a swivelling wrist and circular movements.
- (TT) Swivel the wrist from side to side to align the hand behind the playing finger. Discourage the hand from *rotating* outwards when playing the fifth finger. Students can repeat the third and fourth notes of each bar to exercise the weaker fingers.

  'Gigue' (bars 8 and 16): Students with very small hands may play the left hand arpeggios *non-legato*.
- (RP) Cornelius Gurlitt: 'Study in A minor' (complete)
  Louis-Claude Daquin: 'Suite de la Réjouissance' from *Premier livre de pièces de clavecin* (left hand).

Page 19 **More rounded movements**

- (R) Circular movements (Level 2, p. 12).
- (LO) To combine rounded movements with moving around the keyboard.
- (TT) In all these exercises, the left wrist moves in a clockwise elliptical motion and the right wrist anticlockwise. The arm movement ensures that the forearm is always in line with the playing finger. Start with large movements, then make them smaller and neater, so the thumb still plays on its corner.
- (RP) Heinrich Wohlfahrt: 'Patterns' (No. 10) from *Kinder-Klavierschule*
  Cornelius Gurlitt: Op. 82 No. 53

Page 22 **Thumb on a black note**

- (LO) To develop familiarity with playing with the thumb and fifth finger on a black note.
- (TT) 'Whimsy' can be taught by rote, starting with the left-hand chords. This technique is explored further in 'Broadway' on p. 55, bars 72–77.

Page 23 **Sound explorer**

- (LO) To develop the student's imagination and sensitive listening.
  To encourage exploration of the technical relationship between touch, dynamics and tone colour.
- (TT) These exercises are just starting points for exploring the piano sound more creatively. You and the student can continue to develop similar exercises.

Page 24 **Matching hands**

- **LO** To match sounds between the hands through careful listening.
- **TT** When playing melodies which overlap between the hands, there needs to be a fine balance between freedom of movement and keeping sufficiently close to the keys to avoid accented notes.
- **RP** Clifford Poole: 'The Skating Carnival' from *RCM Celebration Series* Level 2
  Lajos Papp: 'The Mill' from 22 *Little Piano Pieces*
  Giuseppe Concone: '24 Preludes' Op. 37 No. 2

Page 27 **Legato-staccato**

- **R** Legato + staccato (Level 1, p. 16).
- **LO** To play hands together with different articulation. To listen to two voices simultaneously. To prepare for playing canons, contrapuntal pieces and 'Calypso' on page 30.
- **TT** Practise initially with exaggerated *staccato*, then minimise the movement.

  Canons: Encourage the student to learn each hand thoroughly with good shaping, to build up an aural and physical memory of the correct movements before playing both hands together. Start by asking the student to play one voice loudly while you follow quietly, then reverse.

  'Calypso': Clap the left hand rhythm by rote first, then repeat the first two bars until the student feels confident with the rhythm and the *legato-staccato*.
- **RP** Elissa Milne: 'Smooth and Crunchy' from *Very Easy Little Peppers*
  Heather Hammond: 'Spooky Wood Hollow' from *Grooves for Piano Dudes*, Book 3
  Konrad Kunz: *200 Short Two-part Canons* Op. 14
  Andrew Marlow: 'Teapot Invention' from *RCM Celebration Series* Level 1
  Renee Christopher: 'Invention in C major' from *RCM Celebration Series* Level 2

Page 31 **Left-hand melodies**

- **R** The elephant walk (Primer B, p. 11); Legato-staccato (Level 2, p. 27).
- **LO** To develop hand independence and an early awareness of the balance of sounds.
- **TT** Focus mainly on encouraging the student to listen attentively to the bass line. Don't be concerned if the student cannot yet consciously control the balance between the hands. Just the effort to listen to the lower voice will provoke an appropriate instinctive response. Students will be encouraged to achieve greater dynamic contrast between the hands in Level 3.
- **RP** Lajos Papp: 'Waltz 1' from 22 *Little Pieces*
  Yvonne Adair: 'The Lost Bone' (No. 9) from *Little Dog Tales*)
  Béla Bartók: 'I love him from afar' (No. 2) from *For Children* Vol. 2
  Hywel Davis (arr.): 'O Waly, Waly' (Grade 2, ABRSM, 2021–2022)

Page 33 **New major scales**

- **R** Scales (Level 1, p. 29–35); Scales in parallel motion (Level 1, p. 39–42).
- **LO** To develop familiarity with the topography of major scales and the *feel* of each scale under the hand. To introduce ergonomic fingerings, which place the hand in the most natural relationship with the white and black notes.
- **TT** For scales which include black notes, place the hand a little further forward so the fingers can reach the black keys, and all fingers remain evenly curved.
- **RP** Ergonomic fingerings may seem strange at first to the teacher, but students pick them up quickly. See also, F is for fingering (Level 1, p. 30).

  For more information about ergonomic fingerings, see *The Art of Piano Fingering: a new approach to scales and arpeggios* by Penelope Roskell.

Page 35 **Expressive scales**

- R Singing phrases (Primer B, p. 15); Thumb under (Primer B, pp. 28–33); Thumb under 4 (Level 1, p. 31); 4 over thumb (Level 1, p. 32); Circular movements (Level 2, p. 12); More rounded movements (Level 2, p. 19).
- LO To combine the skipping-rope technique with flowing arm movements for a very expressive scale. To combine rounded movements within a scale.
- TT The arm hangs loosely as it guides the hand and finger along the keyboard in one continuous flow. Start by teaching very conscious wrist movements. Then just encourage the student to *feel* the natural shape of the phrase.

Page 38 **Alberti bass**

- R Playing legato (Primer A, pp. 35–36); Rotation (Level 1, pp. 53–55). See also *The Complete Pianist*, pp. 277-294.
- LO To develop rotation for *Alberti bass* at different tempi.
- TT Experiment with both gentle and more energetic rotation. Rotate towards the fifth finger, not beyond. An *Alberti bass* can be a useful accompaniment for improvisations. See also *The Complete Pianist*, pp. 277-294.
- RP Béla Bartók: 'Meditation' (No. 45) from *Mikrokosmos* Vol. 2
  'Broadway' (Level 2, p. 54, bars 57–78)

Page 40 **Broken thirds**

- R Alberti bass (Level 2, p. 38).
- LO To play broken thirds with rotational freedom.
- TT Stay balanced on each finger. Do not tip the hand over too far – only rock as far as the next finger, not beyond.
- RP Béla Bartók: 'Broken thirds' (Appendix 9) from *Mikrokosmos* Vol. 2
  Muzio Clementi: Sonatina in C (Level 2, p. 52, bars 7, 13 and 37)

Page 41 **Harmonic minor scales**

- R The A minor scale (Primer B, p. 35)
- LO To develop familiarity with the look, feel and sound of the harmonic minor scales A, D and G.
- TT Position the arm in line with the fourth and fifth fingers, so that the augmented interval is played with ease. The hand should be placed slightly forward, so the fourth finger can reach the G♯ without stretching.
- RP Pam Wedgwood: 'The Snake Charmer' (No. 8) from *Up-Grade! Piano Grades 1–2*
  Anthony Williams: 'The Egyptian Level' from *Spooky Piano Time*
  Cornelius Gurlitt: No. 52 in A minor, Op. 82
  Béla Bartók: 'In Oriental Style' (No. 58) from *Mikrokosmos* Vol. 2
  Renée Christopher: 'The Snake' from *RCM Celebration Series* Level 1

Page 43 **The elbow spa**

- R Circle warm-ups (Level 2, p. 6)
- LO To prepare for playing arpeggios. To soften the elbow so it hangs loosely, ensuring freedom of movement in all directions.
- TT Ask the student to repeat some of these exercises on a regular basis. Keep reminding them to relax their elbow and shoulder when playing arpeggios and other gestures.

Page 44 **One-octave arpeggios**

- (R) Broken chords with inversions (Level 1, p. 48); Expressive scales (Level 2, p. 36); The elbow spa (Level 2, p. 43); Playing with 4 and 5 (Level 2, p. 17).
- (LO) To play smooth, flowing arpeggios with a swinging wrist.
- (TT) Pianists with very small hands may find the stretch of a fourth between the third and fifth finger challenging. They may need to focus on dominant sevenths, or detached arpeggios, before studying the *legato* one-octave arpeggio. Aim to keep the hand compact to avoid unnecessary stretches between the fingers. Use a flexible swivelling wrist to keep the arm in line with the playing finger, but don't swivel too far. Keep the elbow relaxed – this is primarily a wrist movement.
- (RP) 'Broadway', p. 54, bars 1–6
  Ludovico Einaudi: 'Elegy for the Arctic' and 'Experience' (from *Einaudi Graded Pieces for Piano Grade 1–2*)
  Cornelius Gurlitt: Op. 82 No. 80
  Giuseppe Concone: Op. 24 No. 18

Page 47 **Crossing hands**

- (R) Leaps and bounds (Level 1, p. 43)
- (LO) To gain confidence in moving quickly and freely around the whole keyboard.
- (TT) Encourage freedom of movement over and above accuracy initially.
  'Loading Screen': Students can learn this piece by rote. They will need to memorize the notes to be able to look at the keyboard.
- (RP) Boris Berlin: 'The Merry-Go-Round'
  Anne Crosby Gaudet: 'Angelfish'
  June Armstrong: 'D for Daydream'
  William Gillock: 'Fountain in the Rain'

Page 48 **Pedal explorer**

- (LO) To explore the function of the sustaining pedal and its relationship with the sound.
- (TT) Ensure that the heel stays firmly on the floor. Pivot the foot from the ankle while keeping the toes in contact with the pedal. The leg should stay relaxed. If the student can't yet reach the pedal, they could either stand up for these exercises or use a 'pedal extender'.

Page 49 **Legato pedalling**

- (LO) To introduce simple legato pedalling. Good pedalling taught at this level will avoid a lot of confusion later.
- (RP) 'Broadway', p. 54, bars 1–6; 78–98
  Wynn-Anne Rossi: 'Atacama Desert' from *RCM Celebration Series* Level 2, Sixth Series
  Peter Sculthorpe: 'Singing Sun' from *A Little Book of Hours*
  June Armstrong: 'Coral Reef' from *Sea World*
  More advanced:
  Victoria Proudler: 'The Ice Castle' from *Piano Grades are Go!*
  Friedrich Burgmüller: 'Angels' Voices', Op. 100 No. 21

Page 52 **Combining techniques**

- (LO) Students who have already studied all the techniques in this book will be surprised and delighted to find both the 'Sonatina' and 'Broadway' easy to master.
- (TT) 'Sonatina': A student who cannot reach the octave comfortably should play bars 20–21 detached.